UNDERSTANDING
SWAP
FINANCE

UNDERSTANDING
SWAP
FINANCE

JOHN F. MARSHALL

Graduate School of Business
St. John's University, New York

KENNETH R. KAPNER

Hongkong and Shanghai Banking Corporation

FN75AA
PUBLISHED BY
SOUTH-WESTERN PUBLISHING CO.
CINCINNATI, OH   WEST CHICAGO, IL   DALLAS, TX   LIVERMORE, CA

1 2 3 4 5 6 7 M 4 3 2 1 0 9

Printed in the United States of America

Marshall, John F.
    Understanding swap finance / John F. Marshall, Kenneth R. Kapner.
        p.   cm.
    Includes bibliographical references.
    ISBN 0-538-81024-6
    1. Swap (Finance)   I. Kapner, Kenneth R.   II. Title
HG3881.M335   1990
658.15'99- -dc20   89-19703
                                                                   CIP

FOREWORD

Since the inception of Currency Swaps in the late 1970s and Interest Rate Swaps in 1981, the market for swaps has exploded to the point that the U. S. dollar interest-rate swap curve is considered by some to be second only to the U. S. Treasury term structure in significance. When we began the decade of the eighties, capital market issues were rarely swapped; while now, it seems noteworthy if an issue is not swapped! The volume of new swaps increased from a few hundred million dollars in 1981 to over $550 billion in 1988. Related products, such as Caps and Floors, have developed rapidly as variations on the basic swap structure. Indeed, the market, now known variously as the Derivative Products or Swaps Market, has come to symbolize innovation in the financial markets in the 1980s.

The internationalization of the currencies of the Swaps Market has been a key determinant in its exponential growth. While the dollar has maintained its dominant position for interest-rate swaps, it increasingly shares the spotlight with, amongst many, Deutsche marks, Yen, Sterling, and Canadian, Australian, and New Zealand dollars.

One of the most significant and often overlooked forces behind the the market's growth has been the advent of the personal computer. In the days of calculators and accountant's spreadsheets, it was a monumental task to price and reprice a complex transaction, especially one involving more than two parties and a volatile rate environment. Indeed, early practitioners would often say, "Three-way deals don't close." Personal computers, like the Apple II and the IBM and its compatibles, provided a dramatic impetus to the market by making the necessary computations far less formidable and providing the speed to perform the calculations and effect transactions while prices are still current.

The financial press has covered the development of swaps closely since its inception, and authors with practical, legal, accountancy and theoretical backgrounds have sought to explain its complexities. In this book, Jack Marshall and Ken Kapner have provided a very thorough primer for the beginning student of swaps. The book provides a conceptual and a practical framework for grasping this seemingly complex field. The authors make it clear that swaps need not be thought of as intricate or difficult if one understands the basic concepts that are the essential building blocks and remembers that all elaborate structures can ultimately be reduced to basic components.

A trick to utilize in learning about swaps as you work your way through this book is to keep a pencil and a pad available so that you may draw the boxes, arrows, and cash flows which are essential to this trade. Work through the numbers with the authors and confirm each step in their calculations.

Robert J. Schwartz, Jr.
Senior Vice President
Capital Markets Group
The Mitsubishi Bank, Ltd.

PREFACE

No other markets have ever grown or evolved as rapidly as have the swap markets. This is a testament to the efficacy and flexibility of the instrument, the resourcefulness and the professionalism of the new breed of financial engineer, and the increased appreciation by financial managers of the importance of risk management in a volatile interest-rate and exchange-rate environment. The swap markets have proven very adaptable. The original swap products, now known as "plain vanilla" swaps, have given way to dozens of different variants designed to serve very special purposes. Swaps are now used by industrial corporations, financial corporations, thrifts, banks, insurance companies, world organizations, and sovereign governments. They are used to reduce the cost of capital, manage risks, exploit economies of scale, arbitrage the world's capital markets, enter new markets, and create synthetic instruments. New users, new uses, and new swap variants emerge almost daily. Clearly, it is difficult to overstate the importance of the swap markets to modern finance.

More than any other modern markets, the swap markets are dependent upon the existence and liquidity of other markets. These other markets include the market for corporate debt, the market for U. S. Treasury debt, the futures and options markets, the cash markets, and the forward markets. It is not surprising then that the explosive growth in swap volume has been accompanied by enormous growth in trading volume in these other markets. Today, if one wants to understand these other markets, one cannot ignore the impact of the swap market—both as substitutes for other instruments and as complements to them.

When we began work on this book in 1987, there was considerable interest in swaps among the banking community. The financial press that services this industry was publishing numerous articles on various aspects of the swap product and its evolution. There was little interest, however, on the part of the academic community. Few articles appeared in academic journals, little or nothing was available in the way of pedagogically sound and reasonably complete academic tools, and few college courses yet existed which paid serious attention to swaps. We felt that this deficiency needed to be addressed, and so we undertook to write this book. We have attempted to balance theory with practice—a goal which can largely be explained by the mix in the authors' backgrounds.

Although we have written this book for an academic audience, we have not neglected the industry reader. A "trade version" of our book is available from MicroApplications (telephone: 516-821-9355; address: P.O. Box 43, Miller Place, NY 11764). The trade version discusses additional issues of importance to practitioners. In particular, it provides a more detailed examination of other risk management tools (FRAs, FXAs, rate caps, rate floors, etc.) which are often used in conjunction with swaps. The trade version also includes the full text of the ISDA-developed swap code.

While swap structures are complex, they are founded on relatively simple concepts. The complexity can actually be decomposed into a series of elementary components. How these individual components are combined determines the end product. By building up from the bottom, we believe that the swap product can be made understandable—even to a novice. The reader of this book is expected to have a reasonable grounding in financial theory. In particular, the reader should be familiar with present value arithmetic and standard statistical concepts associated with measuring risk and return in an uncertain world.

We do not want to leave the mistaken impression that swaps are easy. They are not. This is not a book to be read lightly. If the book is to serve the purpose for which it is intended, the reader must work his or her way through it. This is especially true for Chapters 3 and 4. Take paper and pen and run through each example we use. Try out each computation before proceeding. Take the time and work some of the end-of-chapter problems.

Since we first started this book, the paucity of academic literature has given way to a veritable flood. Much of this literature, however, is still in the academic pipeline awaiting publication. We refer to much of the published academic literature and a considerable amount of trade literature. For the most part, however, we have relegated our references to these literatures to footnotes and end-of-chapter suggested readings. We did not want to get bogged down in long literature recitals. To help the reader pick up the vernacular of the trade, we have bold faced important terms the first time they appear or when they are first defined. Some important terms are bold faced in more than one chapter.

One of the major problems we have had in writing the book is keeping it current. The markets have evolved so quickly that developments taking place in 1987, which seemed to clearly point to the future of the markets, were old and discarded by the time we neared completion. We have benefited more than we can possibly say from industry practitioners who have commented on various drafts of the manuscript. These include Ravi Mehra and Steve Katz of Marine Midland Bank, and Craig Messenger of Shearson Lehman, Inc. Our special thanks go to Bob Schwartz of The Mitsubishi Bank. Bob's readings of the several drafts of the manuscript and his detailed comments and suggestions have proven invaluable. We are also indebted to the International Swap Dealers Association which accommodated all of our requests for information and to its officers and directors, some of whom read and commented upon portions of the manuscript. We would also like to thank several persons who have asked to remain anonymous. Their comments were no less valuable. Reviews and comments from members of the academic community have also been extremely helpful. In particular, we would like to thank Dr. Kevin Wynne of Pace University and Dr. Vipul Bansal of St. John's University. Any errors that may remain are, of course, entirely our own.

Jack Marshall
Graduate School of Business
St. John's University, New York

Ken Kapner
The Hongkong and Shanghai Banking Corporation

ABOUT THE AUTHORS

John F. Marshall is an Associate Professor of Finance in the Graduate School of Business at St. John's University, New York. He holds the M.B.A., M.A., and Ph.D. degrees. He teaches courses in corporate finance and investment finance. Dr. Marshall is a risk management specialist and serves as a consultant to several major Wall Street firms. He has written extensively on futures, options, and swaps as risk management tools.

Kenneth R. Kapner is Vice President of Domestic Treasury for the Hongkong and Shanghai Banking Corporation. He holds the M.B.A. degree. Mr. Kapner has extensive trading experience in both the foreign exchange and money markets and is a frequent user of the swap product for the hedging of his bank's positions.

CONTENTS

CHAPTER 1

AN OVERVIEW OF THE SWAP PRODUCT

Overview

In this chapter, we introduce the interest rate and currency swap products in what are often called their **plain vanilla** forms. That is, we look at the simplest types of swaps—unencumbered by any of the many special provisions that are often worked into the "terms and conditions" of these products. We begin with a definition of a swap and then briefly examine the history of the swap markets, the fundamental economic principles on which swap activity rests, the basic structure of currency and interest-rate swaps, and the institutional parties involved in swaps together with these parties' reasons for engaging in swap activity.

The Swap Product Defined

A **swap** is a contractual agreement evidenced by a single document in which two parties, called **counterparties,** agree to make periodic payments to each other. Contained in the swap agreement is a specification of the currencies to be exchanged (which may or may not be the same), the rate of interest applicable to each (which may be fixed or floating), the timetable by which the payments are to be made, and any other provisions bearing on the relationship between the parties. Financial swaps are of two major types: **interest-rate swaps** and **currency swaps;** although there are many variants of each. Currency swaps were introduced first, but interest-rate swaps account for the bulk of today's swap activity.

The most common type of interest-rate swap is a **fixed-for-float-ing rate swap**. In this type of swap, the first counterparty agrees to make fixed-rate interest payments to the second counterparty in exchange for floating-rate interest payments to the first counterparty by the second counterparty. The fixed rate of interest is called the **swap coupon**. The interest payments are calculated on the basis of a hypothetical amount of principal called **notional principal**. The notional principal is not exchanged. Only the interest payments are exchanged. If the counterparties' payments to each other coincide, then only the **interest differential** between the two counterparties' respective commitments needs to be exchanged. This "no frills" swap is the basic or "plain vanilla" interest-rate swap. Variants of this basic structure include zero coupon-for-fixed and floating-for-floating interest-rate swaps.

In the basic currency swap, the two counterparties agree to an immediate exchange (technically a sale) of one currency for another at some exchange rate; this exchange rate is usually the current **spot rate**.[1] These currencies are later swapped back (repurchased) at the same exchange rate. In the interim, the counterparties exchange interest payments. In the most common currency swap, one counterparty pays a fixed rate of interest and the other pays a floating rate of interest. This basic currency swap is called an **exchange of borrowings**. As with interest-rate swaps, many variations on the basic currency swap are possible. For example, the currencies may be (1) exchanged in installments together with interest in such a fashion that no final reexchange of principal is required, (2) the agreement may require that the reexchange take place in installments rather than as a single transaction, or (3) the agreement might involve floating-for-floating or fixed-for-fixed rates.

Swap contracts are tailor made to meet the needs of the individual counterparties. As such, they are created with the aid of swap specialists who serve either or both the roles of broker and market maker. As tailor-made contracts, swaps trade in an **over-the-counter** (OTC) type environment—as opposed to the organized exchanges on which highly standardized contracts like futures and listed options trade.

The Origins of the Swap Markets

An **exchange rate** (foreign exchange rate) is the number of units of one currency that can be purchased for one unit of another currency. These rates became extremely volatile in the early 1970s

following the collapse of the **Bretton Woods Agreement.**[2] This exchange rate volatility created an ideal environment for a swap-like
instrument that could be used by multinationals to hedge long-term
foreign exchange commitments. Nevertheless, the first swaps were
created for an altogether different purpose and only later were the
cost-reducing and risk-management uses of these instruments recognized.

Swaps were a natural extension of **parallel loans** and **back-to-
back loans** which originated in the United Kingdom as a means of
circumventing foreign-exchange controls designed to prevent an
outflow of British capital.[3] Throughout the 1970s, the British Government imposed taxes on foreign-exchange transactions involving
its own currency. The intent was to make the outflow of capital more
expensive in the belief that this would encourage domestic investment by making foreign investment less attractive. The parallel loan
became a widely accepted vehicle by which these taxes could be
avoided. The back-to-back loan was a simple modification of the
parallel loan, and the currency swap was a simple extension of the
back-to-back loan. Parallel and back-to-back loans involve two separate loan agreements; each of which exists independently of the other.
Swaps, on the other hand, are created via a single agreement. As we
shall show later, this difference is crucial.

We will illustrate parallel and back-to-back loans by way of a simple
example. We begin with the parallel loan—which involves four parties. Suppose that there is a parent company domiciled in England
having a subsidiary in the United States. Call this firm the British
parent. Suppose further that there is a second parent company, this
one domiciled in the United States, having its own subsidiary in
England. Call this firm the American parent. Now assume that the
U.S. subsidiary of the British parent is in need of U.S. dollar (US)
financing for a period of T years. In the absence of foreign-exchange
controls, the British parent would simply borrow pounds sterling (BP)
in its domestic market for a term of T years and exchange the pounds
obtained for dollars at the current spot exchange rate. The British
parent would then transfer the dollars to its subsidiary in the United
States. For numerical illustration, we will assume that the British parent
can borrow pounds in England at a rate of 9 percent.

Suppose now that the government of England imposes a stiff tax
on currency translations. If the British parent converts pounds to dollars, the government will tax the transaction. This tax is prohibitive,
and it encourages the British parent to search for an alternative way
of obtaining financing for its U.S. subsidiary. One obvious solution
is for the subsidiary to borrow in the U.S. capital markets on its own.

Unfortunately, the subsidiary is not well-known in the United States and, hence, the markets impose a substantial risk premium on its debt. In the extreme, the subsidiary may find the U.S. capital markets completely closed to it. We will assume that the capital markets are open, but the cost of funds is quite high. For purposes of numerical illustration, we will suppose that the American subsidiary of the British parent can borrow dollars in the United States at a rate of 12 percent.

As it happens, the American parent company finds itself with the mirror image problem of the British parent company. That is, its own subsidiary in England requires British pound financing. The American parent has the same options available to it as does the British parent. It can borrow in the U.S. capital markets and exchange the funds so obtained for pounds and then transfer the pounds to its British subsidiary. We will assume that the American parent can borrow in the United States at a rate of 10 percent. But again, controls on currency flows render this option unattractive. Alternatively, the British subsidiary of the American parent can borrow on its own in the British capital markets. Suppose that the British subsidiary of the American parent can borrow pounds directly (in England) at a rate of 11 percent.

Assuming that each subsidiary borrows on its own, the cost of funds to the American subsidiary of the British parent is 12 percent (US), and the cost of funds to the British subsidiary of the American parent is 11 percent (BP). If the two parent companies were to recognize that they have parallel financing requirements, they can simultaneously solve each other's problem. In the process, they can reduce each other's borrowing costs; and they can avoid foreign-exchange taxes. The solution is for the British parent to borrow pounds in England and then lend the proceeds to the American parent's British subsidiary at the British parent's own cost (9 percent). At the same time, the American parent would borrow dollars in the United States and then lend the proceeds to the British parent's American subsidiary at the American parent's own cost (10 percent). The end result is that the British parent's American subsidiary obtains dollar financing at 10 percent (a 2 percentage point savings), and the American parent's British subsidiary obtains pound financing at 9 percent (again a 2 percent savings).

We need to consider the cash flows between the parties. To facilitate this discussion, we divide the term of the loans into three distinct periods. The first period represents the point of the initial transaction ($t = 0$), at which time the initial lending takes place. The second represents the period between time 0 and time T during which the two subsidiaries pay interest to each other's parent firm. The final period represents that point in time ($t = T$) when the principal sums are repaid and the loan obligations are retired. The cash flows for these three periods are depicted in Exhibits 1.1, 1.2, and 1.3, respectively.

Notice that each parent company has obtained for its subsidiary the funds that the subsidiary required. This securing of funds was accomplished without cost to either parent since the parent companies are, individually, borrowing and lending the same sums at the same rate. The parent firms are borrowing from third-party lenders (investors). Since no currencies are exchanged, no currency-translation taxes are imposed on the parallel loans.

The back-to-back loan is very similar to the parallel loan. The main difference is that there are only two parties involved, since the lendings take place between the parent companies directly. In this arrangement, the British parent agrees to lend the American parent pounds, and the American parent agrees to lend the British parent dollars. As before, we assume that the British parent lends to the American parent at the British parent's own cost and that the American parent lends to the British parent at the American parent's own

EXHIBIT 1.1

INITIAL EXCHANGE OF PRINCIPALS
PARALLEL LOAN

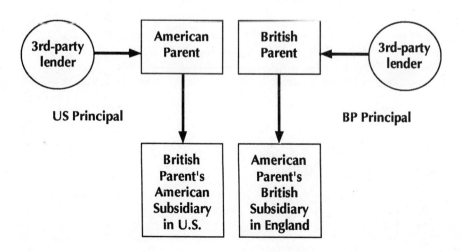

EXHIBIT 1.2

DEBT SERVICE BETWEEN EXCHANGES OF PRINCIPALS
PARALLEL LOAN

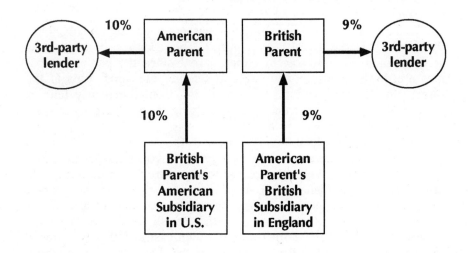

EXHIBIT 1.3

REEXCHANGE OF PRINCIPALS
PARALLEL LOAN

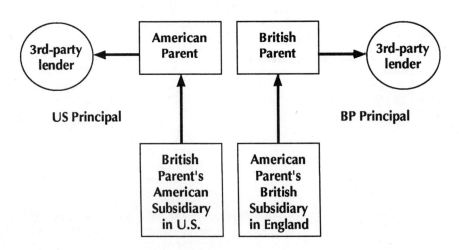

cost. During the term of the loans, each company makes interest payments to the other. At the maturity of the loans, each company repays the principal it borrowed. The cash flows for the three periods are depicted in Exhibits 1.4, 1.5, and 1.6.

There are two problems with back-to-back and parallel loans which limit their usefulness as financing tools. First, a party with a use for this type of financing must locate another party having mirror image financing requirements—called **matched needs**. These requirements include the loan principal, the type of interest to be applied (fixed or floating), the frequency of the coupon payments, and the term of the loan. The **search costs** associated with finding such a party can be considerable—assuming it is even possible. Second, both the parallel and back-to-back loans are actually two loans involving two separate loan agreements. In the case of the back-to-back loan, the British parent's debtor/creditor relationship with the American parent is independent of the American parent's debtor/creditor relationship with the British parent. Thus, if the British parent defaults on its obligations to the American parent, the American parent is not relieved of its obligations to the British parent. This can be very costly for the American parent. To avoid this problem, a separate agreement, defining the **rights of set-off**, must be drafted. If this agreement is not registered, the outcome described above can still occur. On the other hand, registration itself can cause problems.[4]

EXHIBIT 1.4

EXCHANGE OF PRINCIPALS
BACK-TO-BACK LOAN

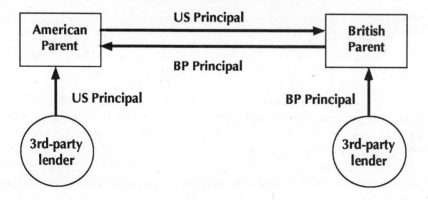

EXHIBIT 1.5

DEBT SERVICE BETWEEN EXCHANGES OF PRINCIPALS
BACK-TO-BACK LOAN

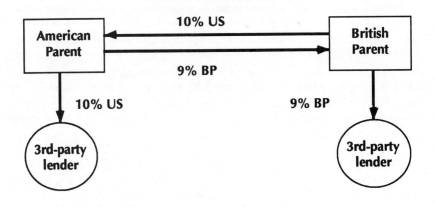

EXHIBIT 1.6

REEXCHANGE OF PRINCIPALS
BACK-TO-BACK LOAN

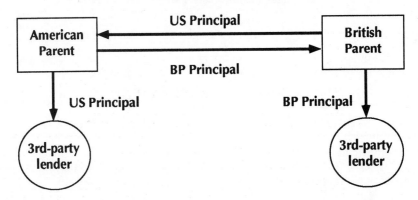

Swaps provide the solution to the rights of set-off problem. The cash flows of the early swaps were identical to those associated with back-to-back loans. However, unlike the two loan agreements that characterize the back-to-back and parallel loans, the swap involves a single agreement. The agreement details all cash flows and provides for the release of the first counterparty from its obligations to the second, if the second counterparty should default on its obligations to the first. This does not, however, prevent either counterparty from seeking damages from the other in the event of one counterparty's default. Thus, with a swap, the American parent's obligations to the British parent terminate if the British parent defaults on its obligations to the American parent. Yet, the American parent can still seek compensation from the British parent for damages to the American parent resulting from the British parent's default.

The other problem associated with back-to-back and parallel loans—finding a party with matched financing requirements—was solved through the intervention of swap brokers and market makers who saw the potential of this new financing technique. We discuss these players shortly.

Although swaps originated from an effort to circumvent foreign-exchange controls, it wasn't long before the cost-reducing benefits of swap finance were recognized. The landmark currency swap, which brought the developing currency swap market from labor pains to actual birth, involved the World Bank and IBM as counterparties.[5] The swap was put together by Salomon Brothers. It allowed the World Bank to obtain Swiss francs and deutsche marks to finance its operations in Switzerland and West Germany without having to tap the Swiss and West German capital markets directly. The stature of the parties involved gave long-term credibility to currency swaps. The market grew rapidly thereafter.

It was a short step from currency swaps to interest-rate swaps. After all, if swaps could be used to convert one type of currency to another at the applicable interest rate on each currency, then why couldn't a similar type of contract be used to convert one type of borrowing (fixed rate) to another (floating rate)? The first interest-rate swap was put together in London in 1981.[6] The interest-rate swap product was introduced in the United States shortly thereafter when, in 1982, the Student Loan Marketing Association (Sallie Mae) executed a fixed-for-floating interest-rate swap.[7]

The economic benefits from swaps can be enormous. Efforts to reap these benefits led to intense utilization of the swap instrument. In the years following the introduction of interest-rates swaps, swap activity exploded. The value of outstanding dollar swaps (currency and interest-rate swaps combined) grew from $5 billion in 1982, to $45 billion in 1984, to $430 billion in 1986. The pace continued to accelerate and by the close of 1987 the dollar swap outstandings totaled $703.1 billion.[8] Of these outstandings, $540.5 billion represented interest-rate swaps, and $162.6 billion represented currency swaps.[9]

When nondollar swaps are added to the total, the year-end 1987 value of outstanding swaps worldwide exceeded the equivalent of $1.1 trillion. As of this writing, final figures for 1988 were not yet available, but all indications are that swap volume has continued to expand. Today, it is not at all uncommon to hear the phrase **"swap driven"** in discussions of capital markets, forward markets, and sometimes futures markets. This is an explicit recognition of the profound effect the swap products have had on these markets. Indeed, the advent of swaps, as much as anything else, transformed the world's segmented capital markets into a single, truly integrated, international capital market.

The Economic Foundations of the Swap Product

The viability of swap finance rests on several important economic principles. The most important of these are the principle of comparative advantage and the principle of offsetting risks. The **principle of comparative advantage** was long ago identified as the theoretical underpinning of international trade.[10] This principle is most easily illustrated in the context of a world having only two economic goods.

Consider two countries which we will call X and Y. Each has 100 inhabitants, and each produces only two goods: wine and cheese. Let's consider each country's annual production possibilities. Suppose that, given their productive endowments, the inhabitants of country X can produce 400 bottles of wine or 200 pounds of cheese or any combination of the two goods that reflects the 2:1 trade-off of wine for cheese. At the same time, given their productive endowments, the inhabitants of country Y can produce 1200 bottles of wine or 300 pounds of cheese or any combination of the two goods that reflects the 4:1 trade-off of wine for cheese. Finally, suppose that the inhabitants of each country find that their utility is maximized when they consume wine and cheese in equal proportions.[11] In the absence of trade, the collective utility of the inhabitants of country X is maximized when the inhabitants of X produce and consume 133 bottles of wine and 133 pounds of cheese. Similarly, the collective utility of the inhabitants of country Y is maximized when the inhabitants of country Y produce and consume 240 bottles of wine and 240 pounds of cheese. It is clear that the inhabitants of country Y enjoy a higher standard of living than do the inhabitants of country X, since both countries have the same number of inhabitants. We also observe that country Y has an absolute advantage in the production of both wine

and cheese. That is, if both X and Y produce just wine, Y can produce more wine per inhabitant. If both X and Y produce just cheese,
Y can also produce more cheese per inhabitant.

Although Y enjoys an **absolute advantage** in both wine and cheese
production, X nevertheless has a **comparative advantage** in the production of cheese. Y, on the other hand, has a comparative advantage in the production of wine. The comparative advantage that X
holds in cheese production stems from X's 2:1 trade-off of wine for
cheese. By giving up two bottles of wine, X can obtain an additional
pound of cheese. If Y gives up two bottles of wine, it will only obtain an additional one-half pound of cheese. It is in this comparative
sense that X holds an advantage in cheese production.

Whenever there are comparative advantages, there is a possibility that both countries can benefit from trade. To see this, suppose
each country concentrates more of its productive resources on pro-
ducing that good in which it holds a comparative advantage and that
all trade between X and Y takes the form of simple barter. For simplicity, we will assume the barter exchange rate is 3 for 1. That is,
three bottles of wine can be exchanged for one pound of cheese. It is
easily shown that the optimal strategy to maximize the collective utility
of the two countries' inhabitants is for X to produce 0 bottles of wine
and 200 pounds of cheese, while Y produces 400 bottles of wine and
200 pounds of cheese. X would then trade 50 pounds of its cheese
for 150 bottles of Y's wine. After this transaction, the inhabitants of
country X have 150 bottles of wine and 150 pounds of cheese while
the inhabitants of country Y have 250 bottles of wine and 250 pounds
of cheese.

Notice that both countries' inhabitants enjoy improved living standards as a consequence of trade. In this specific case, the inhabitants
of country X gained proportionately more than did the inhabitants
of country Y. But both did gain. The extent of each country's gains
from trade will depend on the barter exchange rate and the degree
of comparative advantage that each enjoys.

It is clear that when comparative advantages exist, there can be
benefits to all parties from trade. Whether actual benefits can be realized
will depend on the exchange rate and the **transaction costs**. These
are of paramount importance—both for simple barter and for the viability of the swap market. For purposes of the example, we implic-
itly assumed that wine and cheese could be costlessly traded. That
is, there were no commissions to pay agents for arranging the barter
trade, and there were no transportation costs associated with mov-
ing wine and cheese between X and Y. To the extent that execution
costs exist, the gains from trade will be diminished.

We can easily see that swap finance rests on this same comparative advantage principle. Consider again the currency swap from our
earlier example.   Suppose that the British firm decides to borrow
dollars in the United States to finance its operations in the United
States. As a foreign entity in the United States, the British firm's credit
is not as good as it might otherwise be; and it is forced to pay 12
percent for dollars. In its own country, it can borrow pounds for 9
percent. At the same time, the American firm decides to borrow pounds
in England to finance its operations in England. Again, as a foreign
entity in England, the American firm's credit is not as good as it
might otherwise be; and it is forced to pay 11 percent for pounds. In
its own country, it can borrow dollars for 10 percent. We may sum-
marize as follows:

	Company	
Country	*British Firm*	*American Firm*
England	9.0%	11.0%
United States	12.0%	10.0%

It is clear that the British firm has a comparative borrowing advantage in England and that the American firm has a comparative
borrowing advantage in the United States.   The swap looks to exploit these comparative advantages.   In the swap, the British firm
will borrow in its domestic market at 9 percent and lend the funds
obtained to the American firm at the same 9-percent rate.   At the
same time and as part of the same agreement, the American firm
will borrow in its domestic market at 10 percent and lend the funds
obtained to the British firm at the same 10-percent rate. Thus, the
British firm obtains dollars at 10 percent for a net savings of 2 percent, and the American firm obtains pounds at 9 percent for a net
savings of 2 percent.   Both counterparties to the swap have enjoyed
a gain by exploiting their respective comparative advantages. Of course,
the British firm did not have to lend to the American firm at the
British firm's cost. Nor did the American firm have to lend to the
British firm at the American firm's cost. The gains from the swap
could just as easily have been split unevenly. In either case, if there
are gains to be realized, the swap is viable.
    In banking circles, interest rates are most often quoted in terms
of basis points. A **basis point** is 1/100 of one percent (0.01 percent).
Thus, 2 percent is 200 basis points.   We will often use this convention in our discussion of interest rates, interest-rate spreads, and
interest-rate differentials.

The second principle on which swap finance rests is the **principle of offsetting risks.** Swaps are often used to hedge interest-rate risk and exchange-rate risk. **Interest-rate risk** is the risk that interest rates will deviate from their expected values, and **exchange-rate risk** is the risk that exchange rates will deviate from their expected values. A **hedge** is a position which is taken for the purpose of reducing the risk associated with another position. This risk reduction is accomplished by taking a position having a risk which is opposite that of the original position. The result is that the two risks are offsetting. Thus, hedging involves the principle of offsetting risks.

One of the problems with swaps that we cited earlier is the difficulty of finding a potential counterparty with matching needs. This problem is resolved by swap brokers and other swap professionals working for investment banks, commercial banks, and merchant banks, who locate and match counterparties or, in many cases, actually take one side of the transaction themselves—this is called **positioning a swap** or **booking a swap** and is a function performed by swap dealers (market makers). These swap facilitators (brokers and dealers), as we will call them for the moment, participate in the swap process in exchange for compensation for the services they provide. In the case of the swap broker, the compensation takes the form of a commission. It takes the form of a bid-asked spread and/or an origination fee (called a **front-end fee**) in the case of the market maker (the use of front-end fees has nearly disappeared in recent years except when the swap facilitator is called upon to provide some special financial engineering). If the facilitator's fees are too large, they can wipe out the gains associated with each counterparty's comparative advantage.

The Basic Structure of a Currency Swap

The cash flows associated with the basic currency swap (called an exchange of borrowings) are identical to those associated with a back-to-back loan. The principal difference, as already discussed, is that a currency swap includes termination provisions which relieve a counterparty of its obligations should the other counterparty default. The inclusion of termination provisions makes it unnecessary to detail the rights of set-off in a separate agreement as is typically done with a back-to-back loan.

The currency swap involves three distinct sets of cash flows: (1) the initial exchange of principals (usually obtained by borrowing from third-party lenders—hence, the term "exchange of borrowings"); (2) the interest payments of each counterparty to the other between the exchanges of principals; and (3) the final exchange (reexchange) of principals at the same exchange rate used for the initial exchange of principals. These cash flows are depicted in Exhibits 1.7, 1.8, and 1.9 for a swap involving a British firm and an American firm. The interest rate on U.S. dollars is assumed to be 10 percent, and the interest

EXHIBIT 1.7

CURRENCY SWAP
INITIAL EXCHANGE OF PRINCIPALS

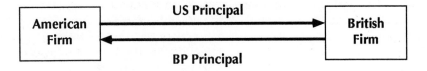

EXHIBIT 1.8

CURRENCY SWAP
CASH FLOWS BETWEEN EXCHANGES OF PRINCIPALS

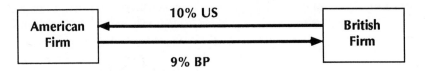

EXHIBIT 1.9

CURRENCY SWAP
REEXCHANGE OF PRINCIPALS

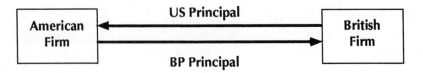

rate on British pounds is assumed to be 9 percent. Thus, this particular exchange of borrowings is a fixed-for-fixed rate currency swap. The most common exchange of borrowings is fixed-for-floating. The floating rate is usually LIBOR but need not be. LIBOR is defined in the next section.

The Basic Structure of an Interest-Rate Swap

There are important differences between currency and interest-rate swaps, and we begin by addressing these. In the "exchange of borrowings" currency swap, there are explicit exchanges of principals at the start of the swap and again at its termination. Both of these exchanges are made at the same exchange rate, which is usually the spot rate prevailing at the time the swap agreement is negotiated. In the interim, the parties exchange interest. These interest payments are made by the payer in the currency of the payee. Thus, there are ongoing full-interest exchanges.

In the plain vanilla interest-rate swap, both currencies are the same. That is, the counterparties are "exchanging" principals in the same currency. Since the principal exchanges are identical and in the same currency, the principal exchanges offset one another and are unnecessary. For this reason, the principal is referred to as "notional." This offsetting of principal exchanges will occur both at the start and at the end of the term of the swap contract. In the interim, the two parties will exchange interest. However, since the interest payments are made in the same currency, they too will be partially offsetting. Therefore, it is only the interest-rate differential which needs to be exchanged in most cases.[12]

In the most common type of interest-rate swap, one counterparty is looking to exchange fixed-rate debt for floating-rate debt, while the other counterparty is looking to exchange floating-rate debt for fixed-rate debt. As an example of a potential counterparty, consider a U.S. savings and loan association (S&L). The S&L has fixed-rate assets (conventional fixed-rate home mortgages) but floating-rate liabilities (time deposits). This mismatch of fixed-rate assets and floating-rate liabilities exposes the S&L to considerable interest-rate risk. There are two ways the S&L can eliminate this risk: (1) convert the fixed-rate assets to floating-rate assets, or (2) convert the floating-rate liabilities to fixed-rate liabilities. Both conversions are possible with properly structured swaps.

Any floating-rate obligation must be tied to some objectively determinable rate which is not easily manipulated by an interested party. This rate could be a short-term lending rate such as the 26-week Treasury bill (T-bill) rate or the prime rate offered by U.S. banks; or the rate could be a longer-term rate such as the 10-year Treasury note (T-note) rate or some average mortgage rate. As a practical matter, however, the rate of choice is usually the **London Interbank Offer Rate** or **LIBOR** for short. LIBOR is a widely recognized rate established daily by a sampling of lending rates offered by leading London banks. The rate is for U.S. dollar lending and originated with the London Eurodollar market. The LIBOR rate most often employed for swap purposes is six-month LIBOR. That is, it is the annual rate applicable on a six-month borrowing of dollars in London. This rate changes daily with fluctuations in the supply of and demand for U.S. dollars. As one would expect, six-month LIBOR is highly correlated with the six-month T-bill rate. All subsequent references to LIBOR are understood to be references to six-month LIBOR unless specifically indicated otherwise.

The second thing to know about interest-rate swaps involving the U.S. dollar is that the fixed-rate side is usually pegged to Treasury note rates. That is, the fixed rate will typically be set at some premium, stated in basis points, to the T-note rate for the note having the same average term-to-maturity as the swap.

Treasury securities are **nonamortizing debt** instruments. That is, the principal is repaid in full at the time of the instrument's maturity. This type of principal repayment is sometimes called a **bullet transaction.** For this reason, swap pricing assumes bullet transactions on the swapped debt. In cases involving **amortizing debt,** the debt's maturity is not directly comparable to the Treasury instrument's maturity. In these cases, it is customary to use average life in lieu of maturity. We discuss this issue in more detail in Chapter 3.

Let's consider an example of the plain vanilla fixed-for-floating interest-rate swap. Suppose Company A and Company B, both of whom are now domiciled in the U.S., have matchable borrowing needs. Company A needs to raise $1 million of five-year money and would like a floating rate. Company A can borrow at a fixed annual rate of 12 percent or at a floating rate of LIBOR plus 2.5 percent. At the same time, Company B needs to raise $1 million of five-year money but wants a fixed rate. Company B can borrow at a fixed rate of 14 percent or a floating rate of LIBOR plus 3.5 percent. Notice that Company A has an absolute advantage in both fixed- and floating-rate borrowings, but Company B, nevertheless, has a comparative advantage in floating-rate borrowings. To see this, simply substitute any percentage for LIBOR and divide the floating rate by the fixed rate. For example, if LIBOR is 8 percent then the ratio of Company B's floating to fixed rate is 11.5% ÷ 14% or 0.821 and the ratio of Company A's floating to fixed rate is 10.5% ÷ 12% or 0.875. Thus, Company B can trade off a "unit" of fixed rate (1 percentage point) for 0.821 units (percentage points) of floating rate, while Company A can trade off a "unit" of fixed rate for 0.875 units (percentage points) of floating rate. Since the goal is to minimize borrowing costs, Company B has a comparative advantage in floating rate. If some value other than 8 percent is substituted for LIBOR, the ratios will be different, but Company B will still have a lower ratio of floating for fixed.

If Company A and Company B can reduce their floating- and fixed-rate borrowing costs, respectively, by entering into a swap, then swap finance is more attractive than straight borrowings. And this is exactly what they can do. If Company A borrows floating-rate money directly, it will pay LIBOR plus 2.5 percent. If Company B borrows fixed-rate money directly, it will pay 14 percent. Now consider the costs to each company if each borrows in the market in which it has a comparative advantage, and then they enter an interest-rate swap. For the moment, we will ignore any costs associated with arranging the swap.

Suppose Company A borrows fixed-rate money from a third party agreeing to pay 12 percent. This is the market in which Company A has a comparative advantage. At the same time, Company B borrows floating-rate money from another third party agreeing to pay

EXHIBIT 1.10

INTEREST FLOWS BETWEEN COUNTERPARTIES
INTEREST-RATE SWAP

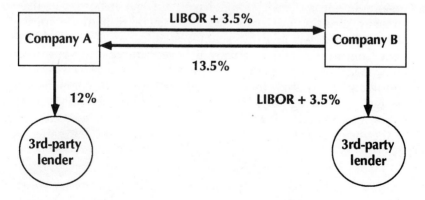

LIBOR plus 3.5 percent. This is the market in which Company B has a comparative advantage. Next, suppose the two companies agree to a swap in which Company B would pay Company A a fixed rate of 13.5 percent on $1 million. This is 1.5 percent more than Company A must pay its third party. At the same time, Company A will pay Company B a floating rate of LIBOR plus 3.5 percent. Since there are no exchanges of notional principal, the only cash flows between the counterparties we need to consider are the interest transfers. These are depicted in Exhibit 1.10. In this exhibit, the flows to the third parties are included as well as the flows between the counterparties to the swap.

Consider first the true cost of Company A's $1 million dollars of five-year money and the form of its *net* interest obligation. Since Company A is receiving 1.5 percent more from Company B than it must pay its third party, it can apply this excess toward the rate it pays Company B; its true interest cost is then LIBOR + 2.0 percent (3.5% - 1.5%). Further, since Company A's fixed-rate commitment to its third party is offset by its fixed-rate receipts from Company B, Company A's only remaining obligation is the floating-rate it pays Company B. Thus, Company A achieved what it wanted, i.e., floating-rate five-year money. Moreover, it has achieved this borrowing at an effective rate of LIBOR plus 2.0 percent (after adjusting for its fixed-rate excess of 1.5%). This rate is 50 basis points less than Company A would have paid had Company A borrowed floating-rate money directly. Now consider Company B's situation. Company B wanted to raise $1 million of fixed-rate five-year money. Although Company B pays a floating rate to its third party, this floating-rate payment is completely offset by the floating-rate payment it receives from Company A. Company B's only real cost is the 13.5 percent fixed rate it pays Company A. Thus, Company B has achieved its objective of borrowing fixed-rate five-year money. Furthermore, Company B is paying 50 basis points less than it would have paid had it borrowed fixed-rate money directly. The costs and net benefit from these transactions are summarized in Exhibit 1.11.

Both Company A and Company B have reduced their borrowing costs through the interest-rate swap, and each has achieved the type of borrowing it required. In this particular case, both companies reduced their borrowing costs by 50 basis points. We should point out that it is coincidental that the two companies enjoyed identical gains from the swap. They could just as easily have split the gains unevenly.

EXHIBIT 1.11

COMPARISON OF BORROWING COSTS WITH AND WITHOUT A SWAP

Without a Swap

Company	Fixed Rate	Floating Rate
A	12.0%	LIBOR + 2.5%
B	14.0%	LIBOR + 3.5%

With a Swap

Company A

Pays fixed to third party	+ 12.0%
Pays floating to B	+ LIBOR + 3.5%
Receives fixed from B	- 13.5%
Net cost to A	LIBOR + 2.0%

Net savings to A = 50 basis points

Company B

Pays floating to third party	+ LIBOR + 3.5%
Pays fixed to A	+ 13.5%
Receives floating from A	- (LIBOR + 3.5%)
Net cost to B	13.5%

Net savings to B = 50 basis points

Suppose now that while Company A and Company B have matching needs, each is unaware of the other. If they are unable to identify each other, the gains from an interest-rate swap will be foregone. Now suppose a facilitator could identify the two parties as having matching needs. Might Company A and Company B be willing to pay something for this service? Suppose the facilitator demanded 75 basis points from each. Would the swap still be attractive? Clearly not. But suppose the facilitator only required 25 basis points from each. In this case, the swap would still be attractive. Thus, the role of the swap facilitator can be justified when the gains from the swap are greater than the transaction costs imposed by the swap facilitator.[13]

Swap Facilitators

In the absence of swap facilitators, there can be very significant search costs associated with finding potential counterparties who have matching needs. This introduces the role and the importance of swap facilitators. We will briefly discuss two types of swap facilitators: brokers and dealers. The financial institutions that serve these roles include investment banks, commercial banks, merchant banks, and independent broker/dealers. We will refer to these institutions collectively as "swap banks" or simply "banks."

Brokers

Financial institutions first became involved in swaps in the role of swap broker. The function of the swap broker is to find counterparties with matching needs. The **swap broker** performs the search to locate parties with matching needs and then negotiates with each on behalf of the other. The service is performed in exchange for a fee called a **commission**. During the search process and during the early stages of negotiation, the swap broker ensures the anonymity of the potential counterparties. Should the negotiations break off, neither party is at risk of having its financial condition divulged by the other. When serving as a swap broker, the bank assumes no risk, since it is not taking a position in the swap. Its role is limited to that of agent.

When the swap technique was first developed, the potential gains from swaps were often considerable. Gross benefits sometimes amounted to several hundred basis points. In such an environment, the brokers who arranged swap transactions could command significant fees. But, as the swap market attracted an ever growing number of participants, much of the potential cost-saving gains from swap finance were arbitraged away. This did not diminish the risk-management uses of swaps, but it did create a need for a more efficient and streamlined swap product. Financial institutions soon created such a product. In the process, they discovered their own potential as a market maker by assuming the role of a counterparty.

Dealers

The trick to streamlining the swap process and standardizing the swap product is for the bank to transform itself from a broker into a dealer or market maker. The **swap dealer** stands ready to match any client's currency or interest-rate requirements by offering itself as the counterparty to the swap. In order to limit its risk, the dealer must be able to lay-off the swap in another swap, called a **matched swap,** or in some standardized form of debt or its equivalent. We focus, for the moment, on the latter.

The broadest debt market in the world is the market for U.S. Treasury securities. The market for Treasury debt is made by U.S. Government securities dealers. These dealers make a market in short-term T-bills, intermediate-term T-notes, and long-term T-bonds. Because of the breadth and the immense volume of trading activity, this market is very liquid; and the **bid-asked spread** is typically very narrow (the bid-asked spread is the difference between the bid price and the asked price). Further, at any given time, there is a near virtual continuum of Treasury maturities, ranging from a few days to thirty years. It is not surprising that the Treasury market was the market of choice for laying-off the dealer's swap risk. Also, it explains why swap dealers price their product as a spread over Treasuries having maturities matching the average life of the swap.

Consider a simple example involving a swap bank and an interest-rate swap. Each morning, the bank's swap staff prepares an **indicative swap pricing schedule.** This schedule specifies the prices at which the bank will enter into swaps for that day. Examine the pricing schedule in Exhibit 1.12 which provides prices for five-year fixed-rate money.

EXHIBIT 1.12

INDICATIVE SWAP PRICING SCHEDULE
(01 June 1989)

Maturity	_Bank Receives_	_Bank Pays_
5 years	TN rate + 80 bps SA	TN rate + 60 bps SA

N.B. All quotes are against six-month LIBOR flat and assume bullet transactions. For amortizing loans, substitute average life for maturity.

These rates are interpreted as follows: The bank will pay the counterparty client **LIBOR flat** (meaning without a premium or discount) in exchange for the counterparty client paying the bank the five-year T-note rate plus 80 basis points. If the counterparty client wants to receive the fixed rate rather than pay the fixed rate, the bank will pay its counterparty client the five-year T-note rate plus 60 basis points in exchange for the client paying the bank LIBOR flat. The bank makes its profit from the bid-asked spread that is easily seen to be 20 basis points. In addition, the bank might charge the client a front-end fee.

Assume the current five-year T-note rate is 9.15 percent. The bank will receive 9.95 percent or pay 9.75 percent against LIBOR. Suppose now that the bank's client can issue (sell) fixed-rate five-year debt at 11.50 percent and can issue floating-rate five-year debt at LIBOR plus 1.50 percent. The client would like to raise $1 million of five-year fixed-rate money. If the client borrows in the fixed-rate market, it will pay 11.50 percent. The bank suggests that the client issue $1 million of floating-rate money at LIBOR plus 1.5 percent and then swap this floating-rate debt for fixed-rate debt with the bank serving as the counterparty. In this swap, the bank will pay its counterparty client LIBOR, and the counterparty client will pay the bank 9.95 percent. There is, as pointed out earlier, no need for the client and the bank to exchange principals, since the principal sums are identical. The cash flows then look as depicted in Exhibit 1.13.

Observe that the counterparty client is paying the third-party lender LIBOR plus 1.5 percent, but the bank is paying the counterparty client LIBOR flat. At the same time, the counterparty client is paying the bank 9.75 percent. Thus, the counterparty client's actual cost for its $1 million of five-year money is 11.45 percent (9.95% + LIBOR + 1.5% - LIBOR).[14] Had the client borrowed fixed-rate five-year money directly, it would have paid 11.50 percent. Thus, the swap strategy has saved the client 5 basis points.

By entering into the swap, the swap bank has assumed the risk that the interest rate it pays the client will change. This interest-rate risk exists because the bank is paying a floating rate. The ideal solution for the bank is to enter into another swap with another counterparty client who seeks to exchange fixed-rate debt for floating-rate debt. If such a party is found, the bank can be viewed as standing between the two counterparty clients in the traditional sense of a **financial intermediary.**

Suppose that it might take some time for the swap bank to locate a second counterparty client. How can the bank lay-off the risk in the interim? The answer is to short $1 million of five-year T-notes and use the proceeds from this sale to purchase $1 million of 26-week T-bills. If it were necessary to do so, the bank would roll these bills over every six months for five years. The T-bill rate is viewed as floating in that it will be different with each **rollover.** This is the same sense in which the LIBOR rate is floating. The bank is then paying a fixed-rate (T-note) and receiving a floating rate (T-bill). The bank's interest-rate risk from the swap with its counterparty client is thus offset. Importantly, the offset is not perfect because the floating-rate side of the swap is LIBOR based, while the Treasury hedge is T-bill based. While these two rates track each other very closely, they are not perfectly correlated, and thus there is some residual risk associated with the hedge. This risk is called basis risk.

EXHIBIT 1.13

INTEREST-RATE SWAP WITH MARKET MAKER BANK CASH FLOWS

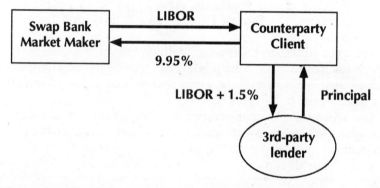

There are other risks for banks making markets in swaps: counterparty credit risk, maturity risk, and several forms of mismatch risk. If the floating-rate portions are indexed to different rates, then there is also basis risk. When the swap involves different currencies, there may be sovereign risk and delivery risk. We save a detailed discussion of these risks and the management of swap risks for Chapter 4.

Some Miscellaneous Points About Swaps

In this section, we briefly consider two important areas involving swaps. The first is the off-balance sheet nature of swaps, and the second is the efforts which have been made to standardize swap agreements.

Swaps are **off-balance sheet** transactions. That is, they do not show up on the asset side or on the liabilities side of a balance sheet. This accounting treatment of swaps has been an attractive feature of swaps to both corporate users of swaps and to swap banks. In particular, swap banks found swap activity to be an easy way to boost bank return on equity—an important measure of profitability. The rapid growth of swap activity eventually led bank regulators to become concerned about bank safety. This led bank regulators to propose regulations which would stiffen capital requirements for such banks.[15] The banks argued that such measures would only increase the cost of swap finance to the end user and drive swap finance overseas.[16]

To address these and related concerns, the Federal Reserve, working with bank regulatory and supervisory bodies from the Group of Ten, developed a preliminary set of proposals which became known as the Basle Accord. The Basle Accord was the culmination of a serious international effort to standardize the measurement of bank capital and to develop capital standards. After a period of public comment and deliberation, the Federal Reserve issued final guidelines for U.S. banks on January 19, 1989.

The Federal Reserve's final guidelines provided a risk-based procedure for determining a bank's capital requirements. The guidelines took explicit consideration of swap and related activity. We address this issue again in Chapter 4.

The second major consideration we briefly address is swap documentation. When the swap product was first introduced, each bank that entered the swap markets as a broker and/or dealer developed its own swap documentation. This documentation included specification of terms, language, pricing conventions, and so on. Different banks used very different terminology and conventions. This lack of standardization limited the ability of banks to assign swaps and slowed the development of a **secondary market** in swap contracts. In June 1985, the New York-based **International Swap Dealers Association (ISDA)** established a code listing standard terms for interest-rate swaps. Shortly thereafter, the **British Banker's Association** offered its own set of documentation guidelines (British Banker's Association Interest Rate Swaps or **BBAIRS**). These codes were later revised and, ultimately, led to the introduction of standard form agreements. The ISDA and BBAIRS alternative codes are referred to, colloquially, by persons in the swap trade as "is da" and "b bears." We address swap documentation and ISDA's efforts toward standardization more fully in Chapter 5.

The standardization of documentation has increased the speed of transacting and given an impetus to the development of a secondary market in swaps. The secondary market continues to evolve but is, as yet, not highly developed. For swaps to be easily tradeable, they would have to be written with **rights of assignment**. Rights of assignment pose a number of difficulties, which we address in Chapter 4. In a related effort, some consideration has been given to the creation of a **clearinghouse** for swaps.[17] Such a clearinghouse could, theoretically, function in much the same fashion as the clearing associations used to clear and enforce futures and option contracts. These efforts appear to have been abandoned, and, in any case, the creation of a clearinghouse for swaps would make swaps too much like futures. This could pose serious regulatory problems for the industry. The absence of a well-developed secondary market for swaps is not, however, a serious problem for swap counterparties. A counterparty to a swap who finds that the swap no longer serves its purposes can negotiate a cancellation of the agreement directly with the other counterparty. We examine the mechanics for determining cancellation payments later.

This concludes our introduction to swap finance. In the next chapter, we consider the uses of swaps and some of the many speciality swaps and swap variants which have emerged in recent years.

Summary

Swap finance evolved from parallel and back-to-back loans. These latter financing devices originated as a mechanism to circumvent foreign-exchange controls. The first swaps were currency swaps, but interest-rate swaps, first introduced in 1981, account for the bulk of swap activity today. Swaps can be used to reduce financing costs and to manage interest-rate and exchange-rate risks.

Swap finance is facilitated by the intermediating roles played by swap brokers and dealers. Brokers arrange swaps between parties with matching needs. Dealers become counterparties to swaps and hedge their positions until such time as matched swaps can be arranged. Large swap dealers often carry swap portfolios measured in the tens of billions of dollars.

The off-balance sheet nature of swaps has led to some concern on the part of bank regulators as to the vulnerability of these financial institutions. Traditional bank accounting and regulation does not provide for explicit recognition of off-balance sheet items and the risks associated with them. This deficiency has been addressed by the Federal Reserve's new guidelines for risk-based capital requirements.

In 1985, the first steps were taken by the International Swap Dealers' Association and the British Bankers' Association toward a standardization of swap provisions and language. This has greatly facilitated the writing of swaps and has enhanced the prospects for the emergence of an efficient secondary market in swaps.

Terms

absolute advantage
amortizing debt
back-to-back loans
basis point
bid-asked spread
Bretton Woods Agreement
British Bankers' Association (BBA)
bullet transaction
clearinghouse
commission
comparative advantage
counterparties
currency swaps
exchange of borrowings
exchange rate
exchange-rate risk
financial intermediary
fixed-for-floating rate swap
front-end fee
hedge
indicative swap pricing schedule
interest differential
interest-rate risk
interest-rate swaps
International Swap Dealers' Association (ISDA)
LIBOR
LIBOR flat
matched needs
matched swap
nonamortizing debt
notional principal
off-balance sheet
over-the-counter
parallel loans
plain vanilla
positioning a swap (booking a swap)
principle of comparative advantage
principle of offsetting risks
rights of assignment
rights of set-off

rollover
search costs
secondary market
spot rate
swap
swap broker
swap coupon
swap driven
swap dealer (market maker)
transaction costs

REVIEW QUESTIONS

1. Briefly discuss the origins of swaps. What advantages do currency swaps have over back-to-back loans?

2. Discuss the comparative advantage justification for the viability of swaps. How might arbitrage affect this comparative advantage?

3. How might swaps be used to hedge interest-rate and exchange-rate risk? Discuss. Illustrate by way of cash-flow diagrams.

4. Why do swap dealers often use the Treasury market to offset their swaps? How does this relate to the pricing of swaps?

5. Why is the principal in interest-rate swaps only notional, while the principal in currency swaps is real?

6. How can swap activity be used to enhance a bank's return on equity? What problems, if any, might this pose for bank safety?

7. What is the rights of set-off problem associated with back-to-back loans, and how is this problem solved by swaps?

8. Distinguish between amortizing and nonamortizing debt.

9. Suppose that a corporation wants to borrow fixed-rate money. It can borrow at a fixed rate of 11.75 percent. Suppose now that this same corporation can borrow floating rate at LIBOR plus 1.80 percent and can enter a fixed-for-floating interest-rate swap with a swap bank. The bank would pay LIBOR flat, and the corporation would pay 9.80 percent. Should the corporation borrow fixed-rate money directly, or should it borrow floating-rate money and swap into fixed-rate money? Why? Illustrate by way of cash-flow diagrams.

10. How might standardization of swap contract documentation facilitate the development of a secondary market in swaps?

ENDNOTES

1. The spot exchange rate is the current rate of exchange for currencies to be paid and received for immediate delivery. As a practical matter, this is usually taken to mean two business days. This is in contrast to forward exchange rates that are current exchange rates for currencies to be paid and received for deferred delivery.
2. For an examination of exchange rate volatility behavior before and after the collapse of the Bretton Woods Agreement, see Wilford (1987).
3. For a discussion of the evolution of swaps from back-to-back and parallel loans, see Powers (1986).
4. For a discussion of the problems which can result from the registration of the rights of set-off, see Price (1986).
5. For an analytical examination of the World Bank's 1981 swap activity, see Park (1984). Also, see Wallich (1984).
6. See Beckstrom (1986) for details of this swap.
7 See Beckstrom (1986).
8. Exact figures for the volume of swap activity do not exist. The numbers reported here for 1982, 1984, and 1986 are our own composites from estimates by Falloon (1988), Celarier (1987), Baker (1986), Powers (1986), and other sources. The figures for 1987 are more accurate. They represent an aggregation of the values provided by reporting members of the International Swap Dealers Association (ISDA), a trade association founded in 1985. The ISDA now tracks the volume of swap activity worldwide. Nevertheless, the 1987 figures are still estimates, since not all swap dealers report their transactions to the ISDA.
9. One has to be careful in tabulating currency swaps because there are always two currencies involved. To avoid double counting, we should divide the currency swap outstandings in half. This has not been done here since only dollar swap outstandings are reported.
10. The principle of comparative advantage, as the driving force behind international trade, was first formulated by David Ricardo in the early nineteenth century. For a more detailed discussion of the principle, see Samuelson and Nordhaus (1985, chapter 38).
11. The term "utility" is used in the economic sense. That is, utility is the benefit or satisfaction that an individual receives or ex-

pects to receive from some available alternative. The alternative is most often taken to mean consumption of some good or some basket of goods.

12. The interest differential is exchanged when the swap payment dates are identical. In some cases, the swap payment dates are mismatched. In these cases, there is a full-interest exchange on the payment dates. We address these cases more fully in Chapter 4.

13. In the language of economics, the swap is profitable for the counterparties if the marginal benefits from the swap exceed the marginal costs of the swap. It is important to note that not all swaps are entered for the purposes of reducing financing costs. Many swaps are created entirely for risk-management purposes. In such a case, a swap may be attractive even if it is not profitable. We discuss this possibility in more detail in Chapter 2.

14. This is actually a simplification, fixed rates are based on a 365-day year using a yield measure called the bond equivalent yield; while floating rates are measured on a 360-day year using a yield measure called the money-market-equivalent yield. Thus, the premium over LIBOR employed in this example is not directly addable to the fixed rate without first making an adjustment. We consider this adjustment in Chapter 3.

15. See, for example, Celarier (1987), Cooper and Shegog (1987), Whittaker (1987), Riley and Smith (1987), Klein (1986), and Felgran (1987).

16. See, for example, Nelson (1986) and Kennrick (1987).

17. For a more thorough discussion of the standardization of swap documentation, see Stoakes (1985a, 1985b), and Genova and Thompson (1988). For discussion of the role of a swaps clearing house, see Crabbe (1986).

REFERENCES AND SUGGESTED READING

Baker, M. "Swaps—Driven Offerings Up." *Pensions & Investment Age*, 14:4, 53-54 (February 1986).

Beckstrom, R. "The Development of the Swap Market." In *Swap Finance*, vol. 1, Boris Antl, ed. (London: Euromoney Publications, 1986).

Celarier, M. "Swaps' Judgement Day." *United States Banker*, 98:7, 16-20 (July 1987).

Cooper, R. and A. Shegog. "An Old-Fashioned Tug-of-War." *Euromoney, Swaps Supplement*, 22-27 (July 1987).

Crabbe, M. "Clearing House for Swaps." *Euromoney*, 345-351 (September 1986).

Falloon, W. "The ABC's of Swaps." *Intermarket Magazine*, vol. 5:5, 25-33 (May 1988).

Felgran, S. D. "Interest Rate Swaps: Uses, Risk, and Price." *New England Economic Review* (Federal Reserve Bank of Boston), 22-32 (November/December 1987).

Genova, D. and D. Thompson "A Guide to Standard Swap Documentation." *Commercial Lending Review*, 3:2, 44-49 (Spring 1988).

Kennrick, R. "Bank Regulators Suggest Control of Swap Volumes." *Asian Finance* (Hong Kong), 13:9, 16-18 (September 1987).

Klein L. B. "Interest Rate and Currency Swaps: Are They Securities?" *International Financial Law Review* (UK), 5:10, 35-39 (October 1986).

Nelson J. F. "Too Good to Last?" *United States Banker*, 97:6, 46-40 (June 1986).

Park, Y. S. "Currency Swaps as a Long-Term International Financing Technique." *Journal of International Business Studies*, 15:3, 47-54 (Winter 1984).

Powers, J. G. "The Vortex of Finance." *Intermarket Magazine*, vol 3:2, 27-38 (February 1986).

Price, J. A. M. "The Technical Evolution of the Currency Swap Product," in *Swap Finance*, vol. 1, Boris Antl, ed. (London: Euromoney Publications 1986).

Riley, W. B. and G. S. Smith. "Interest Rate Swaps: Disclosure and Recognition." *CPA Journal*, 57:1, 64-70 (January 1987).

Samuelson P. A. and W. D. Nordhause. *Economics*, 12d. (New York: McGraw-Hill, 1985).

Stoakes, C. "The London Inter-Bank Swaps Code." *International Financial Law Review* (UK), 4:10, 6 (October 1985a).

Stoakes, C. "Standards Make Swaps Faster." *Euromoney*, 19-21 (November 1985).

Turnbull, S. M. Swaps: A Zero-Sum Game." *Financial Management*, 16:1 15-21 (Spring 1987).

Wallich, C. I. "The World Bank's Currency Swaps." *Finance and Development*, 7:3, 197-207 (Fall 1984).

Wilford, D. S. "Strategic Risk Exposure Management." Working paper #3 in *Working Papers in Risk Management* (Chase Manhattan Bank, February 1987).

Whittaker, J. G. "Interest Rate Swaps: Risk and Regulation." *Economic Review* (Federal Reserve Bank of Kansas City), 72:3, 3-13 (March 1987).

CHAPTER 2

CORPORATE OBJECTIVES AND THE STRUCTURE OF SWAPS

Overview

The structure of a swap is governed by several factors. First and foremost among these is the objective of the end user of the swap product. For purposes of discussion and illustration, we assume throughout that the **end user** of the swap product is a for-profit commercial firm that we sometimes refer to as the corporate user.[1] Also important in determining the structure of a swap is the role played by the financial intermediary, which we continue to refer to as the bank or swap bank. The term "bank" is used generically to include commercial banks, investment banks, merchant banks, and independent swap brokers and dealers. It is reasonable to expect that the bank does all it can to structure the swap so that the swap does, in fact, serve the objectives of the its client the corporate user. To the extent that meeting the client's needs necessitates a swap having an unusually complicated structure or gives rise to a swap that is difficult for the bank to offset, the pricing of the swap will reflect a premium above that which is characteristic of the "plain vanilla" swaps we discussed in Chapter 1. The third major factor affecting the structure of a swap is the laws dealing with the tax and accounting treatment of swaps.

In this chapter, we concentrate on the objectives of the corporate end user of swaps and some of the many swap structures which have been developed by swap banks to meet these objectives. We close with a quick look at some recently developed instruments that can be used as substitutes for swaps or in conjunction with swaps to solve special problems that might face the corporate user.

Corporate Objectives

As shown in Chapter 1, swaps evolved from back-to-back and
parallel loans. Back-to-back and parallel loans involve two separate
loan agreements together with a separate agreement addressing rights
of set-off. These loans were conceived and first used as a mechanism to bypass foreign-exchange controls. While swaps are at least
as useful as back-to-back and parallel loans for purposes of circumventing foreign-exchange controls, this is not now and really never
has been the primary objective of most corporate users of swap products. Far more important to today's corporate users of swaps are (1)
lowering financing costs, (2) hedging price risks (including both
exchange-rate risk and interest-rate risk), (3) operating on a larger
scale, and (4) gaining access to new markets.

Lowering Financing Costs

Imperfections in the world's capital markets create a potential for
the existence of comparative borrowing advantages that, in turn, make
swap finance an attractive financing tool. The imperfections in the
world's capital markets include controls on the movement of capital
across national borders, unequal access to the world's capital markets due to differences in borrower size and market acceptance,
government-granted loan guarantees, differing tax treatments of interest paid and/or received—both internationally and intranationally
—and, finally, different yield curve behaviors in different countries
for both fixed-rate and floating-rate borrowings. In addition to these
obvious imperfections, there are less obvious ones as well. For example, a potential lender may have unequal access to, or knowledge
of, legal protections afforded to lenders in the world's capital markets. Concern over the validity and enforceability of protective covenants can diminish a potential lender's willingness to lend to a nondomestic borrower. The end result is a higher cost of funds for the
nondomestic borrower. Thus, domestic borrowers often enjoy a
comparative borrowing advantage over nondomestic borrowers.

Swap finance can lower borrowing costs for both counterparties
to a swap by exploiting these comparative advantages. We saw how
this can be accomplished with the plain vanilla currency swap and
the plain vanilla interest-rate swap in Chapter 1. With the rapid growth
in swap finance and increasing competition among the banks acting
as swap brokers and dealers, much of the potential cost-reducing
benefits of swap finance have been arbitraged away and market

efficiency has increased. It is for this reason that swap finance has served to integrate and internationalize the world's capital markets.

The substantial narrowing of bid-asked swap spreads, brought about by a general acceptance of swap finance and the standardization of the swap product, may not be beneficial for the less-efficient swap banks (who require more substantial spreads to ensure a profit from their intermediary role). However, it is a financial bonanza for the corporate users of swaps. Through the swap vehicle, such a user can be assured of obtaining funds at the lowest possible cost with minimal expense for the services of the swap banker.

Hedging Price Risks

Of at least equal importance to their use as a tool to lowering financing costs, swaps can be used to hedge financial price risks. Like futures contracts, swaps can be used very effectively to hedge both interest-rate risk and foreign exchange-rate risk. But, whereas futures contracts are best suited to hedging price risks of a relatively short term (typically less than one year), swaps are best suited to hedging price risks of a longer term. These often range from one to ten years and can run considerably longer.

With the extreme volatility which has characterized interest rates and exchange rates, the importance of efficient hedging tools is difficult to overstate. We will illustrate by way of a simple example. Suppose a Swiss provider of retirement annuity contracts sells its policies worldwide. With its most popular policy, the Swiss firm provides fixed quarterly payments to its policyholder (payable at the end of each calendar quarter) for a period of 15 years in exchange for a single immediate payment by the policyholder to the Swiss firm.[2] The Swiss firm does not necessarily invest the funds it receives from its policyholders in the policyholders' country. Rather, the firm looks worldwide for the most attractive investment opportunity it can find.

The Swiss firm is planning a policy offering in the United States. It determines that it can convert any dollars it receives to West German deutsche marks at the current spot exchange rate of 2.000 DM/US and lend these deutsche marks to a German firm at an annual return of 10 percent (compounded quarterly). The loan would be a fifteen-year amortizing loan providing quarterly payments. On the strength of its knowledge of this investment opportunity, the Swiss firm offers its prospective U.S. policyholders a fixed annual rate of 9 percent (compounded quarterly). From the one percent receive-pay rate differential, the Swiss firm must cover its administrative costs and try to earn a reasonable profit for its shareholders. Suppose that the policy offering brings the Swiss firm a total of $50 million from 1,000 new policyholders.

The Swiss firm will receive quarterly revenues from its German investment in the amount of DM 3,235,340.[3] At an exchange rate of 2.000 DM/US, this is equivalent to $1,617,670 for each of the next sixty quarters. At the same time, the Swiss firm must make aggregate quarterly payments to its U.S. policyholders in the amount of $1,526,767. The rate differential then translates, at the current spot exchange rate, to net quarterly revenue of $90,903 or an annual net revenue of $363,612. The Swiss firm estimates that the annual administrative costs associated with providing these policies is $135,000. Thus, if all of its expectations are realized, the new policy offering should contribute $228,612 to the firm's annual profit.

Suppose, for the moment, that the Swiss firm does not hedge its currency commitments. If the deutsche mark strengthens against the dollar, the Swiss firm will profit in excess of its expectations. On the other hand, it will suffer unexpected losses if the deutsche mark weakens against the U.S. dollar. A small adverse change in the value of the deutsche mark could easily wipe out all profit from this offering. For example, if the exchange rate were to rise to just 2.073 DM/US, representing a weakened deutsche mark, the annual profit contribution from the policy offering would be reduced to near zero. A more substantial weakening of the deutsche mark could irreparably impair the financial integrity of the Swiss firm. The effects of an increase in the exchange rate are illustrated in Exhibit 2.1.

The Swiss firm cannot invest globally to earn the best rate possible unless it can hedge its exchange-rate risk. Without this capability, its activities are limited to matching its currency payment commitments by investing exclusively in assets denominated in the currency of its payment commitments (liabilities). Indeed, before the advent of currency swaps, this is exactly what this particular firm did. This strategy is clearly suboptimal. It requires that potentially superior investment opportunities be ignored because of concern over foreign exchange risk. In any case, the Swiss firm is in the business of providing annuity contracts and not in the business of currency speculation and, so, it seeks to hedge its foreign-exchange exposure. The firm often hedges its short-term currency exposures in foreign-exchange forward and futures contracts. But these hedging instruments are not adequate to hedge this multiyear commitment.

The Swiss firm approaches a U.K.-based swap banker for a solution. The banker, which makes a market in both currency and

EXHIBIT 2.1

ILLUSTRATION OF FOREIGN-EXCHANGE EXPOSURE

		—Exchange Rate (DM/US)—		
		2.000	2.073	2.146
Firm receives DM quarterly	DM	3,235,340	3,235,340	3,235,340
Converted to dollars	US	1,617,670	1,560,704	1,507,614
Less US payments to policyholders	US	1,526,767	1,526,767	1,526,767
Gross quarterly profit (US)	US	90,903	33,937	(19,153)
Less quarterly adm. costs	US	33,750	33,750	33,750
Net quarterly profit	US	57,153	187	(52,903)
Net annual profit	US	228,612	748	(211,612)

Note: The actual zero profit exchange rate occurs at 2.0732. For purposes of this example, we treat the second column net quarterly and net annual profits as approximately zero.

interest-rate swaps, offers to pay the Swiss firm dollars at an annual rate of 9.85 percent in exchange for the Swiss firm paying the bank deutsche mark at a 10 percent annual rate. This involves a combination of a fixed-for-floating rate currency swap and a floating-for-fixed interest-rate swap. For both payment streams, we will assume quarterly compounding and a fifteen-year amortizing loan. The loan principal on the dollar side of the swap is $50 million, and the loan principal on the deutsche mark side is DM 100 million. The latter is obtained by converting the dollar side to deutsche marks at the current spot exchange rate.

The Swiss firm now has two separate sets of cash flows. Exhibit 2.2 depicts the cash flows between the German firm, the Swiss firm, and the Swiss firm's U.S. policyholders. Exhibit 2.3 depicts the cash flows from the swap between the Swiss firm and the swap bank.

We can now combine the cash flows depicted in Exhibits 2.2 and 2.3. The *net* cash flows are depicted in Exhibit 2.4.

The Swiss firm is now fully hedged against fluctuations in the DM/US exchange rate. Assuming that the Swiss firm's management has no reason to believe the DM/US exchange rate is more likely to rise than fall in the coming years (that is, the current 2.000 spot DM/

EXHIBIT 2.2

QUARTERLY CASH FLOWS
FROM COMMERCIAL TRANSACTION

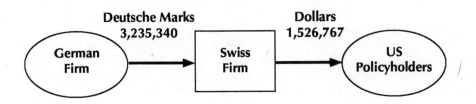

EXHIBIT 2.3

QUARTERLY CASH FLOWS FROM SWAP

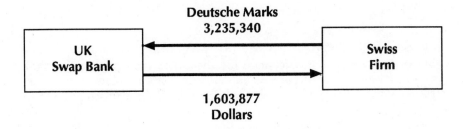

EXHIBIT 2.4

COMBINED CASH FLOWS FROM
COMMERCIAL TRANSACTION AND SWAP

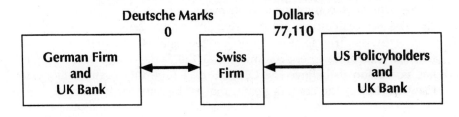

US exchange rate is an unbiased estimate of future spot DM/US exchange rates), the firm's expected annual profit from the policy offering is reduced by the swap hedge to $173,440 [(4 x $77,110) - $135,000].[4] The **cost of the hedge** to the Swiss firm is the amount by which the expected annual profit from the policy offering is reduced as a consequence of hedging. In this case, the annual cost of hedging is $55,172 ($228,612 - $173,440).

It is premature to conclude that the positive hedging costs incurred when hedging with swaps would prevent the Swiss firm from hedging in this instrument. A **risk averse firm** enjoys a utility gain from the risk reduction which accompanies hedging. For this risk reduction, the swap hedger would likely be willing to pay a price—just as futures hedgers are willing to pay a price for the risk reduction made possible by hedging in futures.[5]

There are two ancillary benefits from hedging which are easily overlooked but which should be of considerable importance to the hedger. The first involves reduced financing costs, and the second involves economies of scale.

By hedging, the corporate user of swaps reduces the uncertainty of its cash flows. This has implications for the firm's cost of funds completely separate from the reduced financing costs associated with swap finance itself. By reducing the uncertainty of its cash flows, the firm is viewed as more **creditworthy**. To the extent that the markets recognize this reduction in uncertainty, the firm's cost of debt and equity capital should decline. This, in turn, implies higher prices for the firm's stock.

The second ancillary benefit of hedging cash flows with swaps is associated with the scale on which the firm can operate. This benefit is addressed in the next section.

Exploiting Economies of Scale

Hedging of price risks, including financial price risks, makes it possible for a firm to operate on a larger scale. Consider again the case of the Swiss provider of annuity contracts. The annuity provider that does not hedge cannot operate on the same scale, for a given capital base, as the annuity provider that does hedge. Suppose that the prudent annuity provider holds $1 of equity capital for each $0.40 of annual profit volatility (however this might be defined). Next, suppose that, in the absence of hedging, each $1 of annuity policies

gives rise to $0.05 of profit volatility. The unhedged annuity pro-
vider can then carry, at most, $8 of annuity policies for each $1 of
equity capital it holds.

Now suppose that a complete swap hedge, like the one described
for the Swiss firm above, reduces profit volatility by 90 percent. The
residual risk, called **basis risk**, that remains is then 10% of the risk
which existed in the absence of hedging. The same annuity provider
can then carry $80 of annuity policies for each $1 of its equity capital. Thus, in this example, the hedged annuity provider can operate
on a scale ten times that of the unhedged annuity provider without
bearing any greater risk.

Even when hedging is costly, as it is in the example of the Swiss
firm above, the cost incurred from hedging may be a small price to
pay for the increased scale at which the hedged firm can operate.
The annuity provider that is capable of operating on a larger scale
by hedging, benefits from the greater profits associated with a larger
policy base, but it may also benefit from **economies of scale**. That
is, to the extent that the provision of annuity policies involves a high-
fixed cost and relatively little variable cost per policy, there may be
significant cost savings to be enjoyed by those annuity providers that
can operate on a large scale. These savings alone may be sufficient
in some cases to completely offset the costs of hedging.

Gaining Access to New Markets

There are many ways that swaps allow firms to access markets
that they might otherwise be unable to profitably enter. Consider
just one such possibility. Suppose the Swiss annuity provider would
like to offer its annuity contracts to Italian citizens who require annuity
payments in lira. In the absence of swap opportunities, the Swiss firm,
which cannot afford to take foreign-exchange risk, is limited to finding investment opportunities in Italy. These opportunities might be
inferior to other opportunities in other nations. In fact, given the
investment opportunities in Italy, the Swiss firm might decide that it
cannot currently invest in Italy at a return sufficient to offer Italians
an attractive annuity rate and still earn a reasonable profit. Given
this situation, the Swiss firm judges the Italian market to be closed
to it at the current time.

By engaging a swap banker that makes a market in lira for dollar
swaps, lira for deutsche mark swaps, etc., the annuity provider can

seize an investment opportunity outside Italy and then transform this non-lira asset into a lira denominated asset. With lira assured, the annuity provider can obtain lira financing by offering its policies to Italian citizens in the same way that it offered its policies to U.S. citizens.

There are many other ways in which a firm can use swaps to access markets which would otherwise be closed to it or for which the cost of entering the market is judged to be prohibitive.

Swap Variants

Despite the usefulness of the swap for financing purposes, it is not always acceptable in its plain vanilla form. For example, in the plain vanilla fixed-for-floating interest-rate swap, the corporate user exploits its comparative advantage in the fixed- (floating-) rate market by borrowing in this market and then swaps its payments on this obligation for a more desirable floating- (fixed-) rate obligation. Suppose now that the corporate user can borrow at one floating rate (certificate of deposit rate or commercial paper rate) but prefers to have its liabilities denominated in another floating rate—T-bill or LIBOR, for example. In this case, we require a floating-for-floating rate swap. Or, suppose that the corporate user holds prepayable fixed-rate assets (home mortgages, for example) that are financed with floating-rate liabilities. We can use a swap to convert the fixed-rate assets to floating-rate assets, or we could use a swap to convert the floating-rate liabilities to fixed-rate liabilities. In both cases, we might require a termination option or an option to extend the swap.

One of the important functions that swap bankers perform for their corporate clients is **financial engineering**. While the activities of financial engineers are not new, the explicit recognition of financial engineering as a professional field is quite new. Financial engineering encompasses a variety overlapping areas. For our purposes, we are interested in only one of these areas—the design of customized solutions to the financing and risk-management needs of clients.[6]

Financial engineering requires financial innovation. When a bank custom designs a new swap variant to meet the idiosyncratic needs of a particular client, the bank can charge a significant premium over its own costs for that custom design. This "charge" may take the form of a front-end fee or a wider than normal bid-asked spread on the swap. If this new product has wider appeal however, it will soon be transformed into a standardized high-volume item which will only be profitable for those banks that can deliver it in a very cost efficient manner. The front-end fee will disappear, and the bid-asked spread will narrow. Thus, banks compete against one another to deliver their swap products at the least possible cost; and they depend for the bulk of their profits on a high volume of low margin swap transactions.

The point: Corporate users of swaps often require special features in their swap agreements. Many of these special features have been standardized and have given rise to swaps with special names. We briefly review some of these special types of swaps in the several sections which follow. We look at variant forms of interest-rate swaps first, and then we look at variant forms of currency swaps. All of the swap variants discussed below originated as high-margin custom designs and have since been transformed into low-margin volume products.

Interest-Rate Swaps

The plain vanilla fixed-for-floating interest-rate swap is not adequate to meet the needs of all corporate users. In an effort to better serve the corporate user, innovative banks have created a plethora of variants on the basic fixed-for-floating interest-rate swap. These variants can be used individually or can be combined so that a given interest-rate swap has a number of variant features. Some of the variant forms of interest-rate swaps common today are zero-coupon swaps; floating-for-floating swaps; callable, putable, and extendable swaps; forward swaps; delayed rate-setting swaps; and rate-capped swaps. These and other variants are discussed below.

Fixed-for-Floating Swaps   These are the basic or plain vanilla interest-rate swaps. The corporate user swaps a floating-rate obligation into a fixed-rate obligation or, alternatively, swaps a fixed-rate obligation into a floating-rate obligation. These were the first interest-rate swaps with standardized terms and the first to be offered as a mass-market, low-margin financing tool by swap dealers. The floating-rate side is typically pegged to LIBOR, and the fixed-rate side is typically priced at a spread over the yield on Treasury securities (notes and bonds). In its most common form, the counterparties to the swap make periodic interest payments to each other with the payments made at the same frequency; principal is not exchanged, and exchanges of interest are limited to an exchange of the interest differential—assuming the payment dates and frequencies are matched.

Zero Coupon-for-Floating Swap   This swap is a variant of the fixed-for-floating rate swap. Unlike the usual fixed-for-floating rate swap, in which each counterparty makes payments to the other with the same payment frequency, in the zero-coupon swap the fixed-rate payer makes a single payment at the termination of the swap agreement, with the interest calculated on a discount basis, while the floating-rate payer makes periodic payments. These swaps are attractive to corporate users who themselves hold zero-coupon assets but which pay a floating rate on their liabilities (or vice versa).

Floating-for-Floating Swaps   These are also called **basis swaps**. Floating-for-floating swaps can be of several forms. In one form, the two sides of the swap are tied to different floating rates. For example, one side might be tied to six-month LIBOR; while, the other might be tied to a six-month certificate of deposit or a six-month commercial paper rate. In the second form, the two sides of the swap might be tied to the same pricing vehicle but with different payment frequencies. For example, one side might involve semiannual payments based on six-month LIBOR; while, the other side might involve monthly payments based on one-month LIBOR. A third variant incorporates both of the first two. For example, one side might involve monthly payments priced on one-month LIBOR; while, the other side might involve semiannual payments calculated on six-month certificate of deposit rates. Other rates which have been used to index one side or the other of a floating-for-floating rate swap include prime rate, T-bill rate, and Fed funds rate.

Callable Swaps   A callable swap is a fixed-for-floating swap with a scheduled maturity date but in which the fixed-rate payer (floating-rate receiver) has the right to terminate the swap prior to the swap's maturity date. The fixed-rate payer may be regarded as having purchased a call option on the swap. For the call privilege, the fixed-rate payer typically pays a higher fixed rate than would be paid in a straight fixed-for-floating rate swap and may be required to pay a termination fee in the event the call privilege is exercised. Such a fee is calculated as a percentage of the swap's notional principal.

Putable Swaps   A putable swap is a fixed-for-floating swap with a scheduled maturity date but in which the floating-rate payer (fixed-rate receiver) has the right to terminate the swap prior to the swap's maturity date. The floating-rate payer is regarded as having purchased a put option on the swap. The floating-rate payer pays for the put option privilege by accepting a fixed-rate below that available on a straight fixed-for-floating swap. In addition, there may be an early termination fee payable by the floating-rate payer upon exercise of the option privilege. As with the call option, this fee is calculated as a percentage of the swap's notional principal.

Extendable Swaps   An extendable swap is a fixed-for-floating swap in which one party has the right to extend the life of the swap beyond its scheduled maturity date. These swaps are economically equivalent to callable and putable swaps. For example, an extendable swap in which the fixed-rate payer can extend the scheduled maturity from two years to five years is equivalent to a callable swap with a five-year scheduled maturity but which the fixed-rate payer can terminate after just two years. Like callable and putable swaps, the holder of an option to extend the maturity of a swap will typically have to pay for this valuable right and may have to pay a fee should that right be exercised.

Note: Callable, putable, and extendable swaps can be complimentary from the swap banker's perspective. We postpone discussion of swap complimentarity, however, until Chapter 4.

Forward Swaps   A forward swap, also called a deferred swap, is a fixed-for-floating swap in which the swap rates are set immediately but in which the start of the swap is delayed. This type of swap can be attractive to a corporate user who does not require immediate swap financing but who feels that the prevailing fixed-for-floating rate opportunities are particularly attractive. Through the forward swap, the user "locks-in" the current rate structure but delays the start of the swap until a specific future date.

Delayed Rate-Setting Swaps   Also called deferred rate-setting swaps, delayed rate-setting swaps are a near mirror image of forward swaps. The corporate user is in need of immediate swap financing but considers the current fixed-for-floating rate structure unattractive. The corporate user agrees to enter the swap immediately with the rate to be determined later according to an agreed upon formula.[7] In this type of swap, the corporate user is usually granted the right to set the rates at the time of its choosing within some specified time frame.

Rate-Capped Swaps   Rate-capped swaps are fixed-for-floating swaps in which ceilings are set on the floating rates. That is, the floating rate cannot rise above a certain "ceiling" level, which constitutes the cap. A rate cap affords the floating-rate payer an extra level of protection. For this protection, the floating-rate payer pays the fixed-rate payer a front-end fee. This type of swap is attractive to a corporate user with capped floating-rate assets and fixed-rate liabilities. A mortgage banker holding a portfolio of rate-capped adjustable rate mortgages (ARMs) which are financed by fixed-rate long-term debt would constitute an example of this type of corporate user.[8]

Closely related to the rate-cap swap is the **mini-max swap** that imposes both a floor and a ceiling to the floating-rate side of the interest-rate swap.

Amortizing Swaps   In amortizing swaps, the notional principal on which the interest payments are based gradually declines, usually under a sinking-fund type schedule. The amortization may or may not provide for a grace period on the amortization of the notional principal.

Roller-Coaster Swaps   In roller-coaster swaps, the notional principal on which the interest payments are calculated increases (**negative amortization**) for a time and then amortizes to zero over the remaining life of the swap. The schedule of changes in the notional principal is established at the outset. These swaps can be used by mortgage bankers to hedge portfolios of fixed-rate graduated payment mortgages (GPMs) which are financed by floating-rate liabilities.

Asset-Based Swaps   Most swaps are written to reduce the cost of financing or to hedge existing liabilities. Thus, interest-rate swaps were first designed as a tool for liability management. In recent years, these same swaps have been used to create **synthetic instruments**. A synthetic instrument is a combination of other instruments which behaves exactly like some real financial instrument. These synthetic instruments can be used in arbitrage strategies to exploit price discrepancies between the real asset and the synthetic asset. Such swaps are sometimes called asset-based swaps.

Currency Swaps

Just as the plain vanilla interest-rate swap is not always adequate to meet the needs of an interest-rate swap end user, the plain vanilla currency swap can fail to meet the needs of a currency swap end user. To meet end users' needs, swap banks have created a number of currency swap variants. These variants can be used individually or can be combined with other variants to produce very effective solutions to financing and foreign exchange-risk management problems. We briefly examine the plain vanilla fixed-for-floating rate currency swap, fixed-for-fixed rate currency swaps, floating-for-floating currency swaps, circus swaps, and amortizing swaps. Unlike interest-rate swaps, which do not require an exchange of principals, currency swaps generally do require such an exchange.

Fixed-for-Floating Rate Nonamortizing Currency Swaps   The fixed-for-floating rate nonamortizing currency swap is the plain vanilla form of currency swap. It is often called an **exchange of borrowings**. In this swap, there is an initial exchange of principals at the outset and a reexchange of principals at the swap's termination. Both exchanges are made at the same exchange rate—which is the spot exchange rate prevailing at the time the swap is negotiated. The reexchange of principals at the swap's maturity constitutes the bullet transaction. During the life of the swap, the counterparties exchange periodic interest payments. These payments are most often made annually or semiannually. One counterparty pays interest at a fixed rate, and the other pays at a floating rate with the payments made with equal frequency.

Fixed-for-Fixed Rate Nonamortizing Currency Swaps   The fixed-for-fixed rate nonamortizing currency swap is identical to the fixed-for-floating rate currency swap except that both counterparties pay a fixed rate of interest. This type of swap can be created via a single swap agreement or via two separate swap agreements. In the latter case, a fixed-for-floating rate currency swap can be used for the initial exchange of currencies with the corporate user paying the floating rate. A fixed-for-floating rate interest-rate swap can then be used to convert the floating-rate side to a fixed rate. The end result is a cash flow pattern identical to a fixed-for-fixed rate currency swap.

Floating-for-Floating Rate Nonamortizing Currency Swaps   The floating-for-floating rate nonamortizing currency swap is identical to the fixed-for-floating rate currency swap except that both counter-parties pay a floating rate of interest. This type of swap can be created via a single swap agreement or via two separate swap agreements. In the latter case, a fixed-for-floating rate currency swap can be used for the initial transaction with the corporate user paying the fixed rate. A fixed-for-floating rate interest-rate swap can then be used to convert the fixed-rate side to a floating rate. The end result is a cash flow pattern identical to a floating-for-floating rate currency swap.

Circus Swaps   When a transaction consists of both a currency swap and an interest-rate swap with LIBOR-based pricing for the floating-rate side of each, the swap is called a circus swap. The examples offered above by which a fixed-for-floating rate currency swap is converted to either a fixed-for-fixed or floating-for-floating rate currency swap via a fixed-for-floating interest-rate swap would constitute a circus swap if the floating-rate side of each swap is LIBOR-based.

Amortizing Currency Swaps   Unlike the single reexchange of principals associated with swaps that take the form of bullet transactions, amortizing currency swaps are reexchanged in stages. That is, the principals amortize over the life of the swap. These currency swaps can be fixed-for-floating, fixed-for-fixed, or floating-for-floating.

This look at swap variants is not meant to be exhaustive nor detailed. Other types of interest-rate and currency swaps exist, and new ones are evolving all the time. Our cursory examination of these products is sufficient, however, to provide an appreciation of the versatility associated with these instruments. It is also sufficient to appreciate the complexities associated with pricing these products and the difficulties encountered by swap bankers in managing their swap portfolios.

Related Instruments

There are a number of instruments which are related to swaps in the sense that they can be used for hedging long-term interest-rate and foreign exchange-rate risks and/or to reduce the cost of financ-

ing. These instruments can also be used in conjunction with swaps
to achieve unique solutions to financing and risk-management problems. We briefly consider five such instruments: floating rate notes,
forward rate agreements, foreign exchange agreements, rate caps, and
rate floors.

Floating Rate Notes

Floating rate notes (FRNs) are bond-type debt instruments with
floating-rate coupons rather than the fixed-rate coupons that characterize more conventional long-term debt instruments. The term
"floating rate note" is often used generically to mean any type of
debt security whose coupon is adjusted periodically to reflect changes
in the rate to which the coupon is pegged. These periodic adjustments may be made very frequently, monthly for example, or only
occasionally, once every several years, for example.

Used more narrowly, the term floating rate note is taken to mean
a long- or intermediate-term debt security whose interest rate is pegged
to a short-term rate or rate index and adjusted frequently—more than
once a year. For example, the rate to which these instruments' coupons are pegged might be the prime rate or the 26-week T-bill rate.

FRNs originated in Europe. They first appeared in the United States
in 1973. The U.S. market for FRNs grew rapidly thereafter and, for a
time, demand for these new instruments far exceeded the quantities
offered.[9]

By offering a floating rate note, a corporate issuer can accomplish
the same thing as if it issued fixed-rate debt and then used a fixed-
for-floating interest-rate swap to convert the fixed rate to a floating
rate. It is also equivalent to issuing short-maturity (say 180 days)
commercial paper at the prevailing commercial paper rate and then
rolling this paper over (issuing replacement paper) every six months
at the commercial paper rate prevailing at the time of the rollover.
Which of these alternatives is preferable depends on the all-in cost
of each. **All-in cost** is the total cost of a financial transaction including the interest expense, front-end and/or underwriting fees, periodic servicing fees, etc. This cost is typically stated as a per annum
rate. Consider an example: A domestic corporation provides variable rate financing to purchasers of its products. In order for the
corporation to provide financing to one of its larger customers, it
needs to raise $20 million of new capital. To hedge interest-rate risk,

the corporation would prefer floating-rate financing to fixed-rate financing. The corporation considers the all-in cost of two financing alternatives.

The first alternative is to sell $20 million of floating rate notes. The corporation estimates that the notes can be sold at par if the firm offers a coupon equal to the 26-week T-bill rate plus 1.5 percent. The all-in cost, including the cost of underwriting the issue, is determined to be the T-bill rate plus 1.85 percent.

The second alternative is to sell $20 million of fixed rate notes and then to swap this fixed-rate debt into floating-rate debt. Suppose that the fixed-rate debt can be sold at par with a coupon of 9.25 percent, and that this can be swapped for six-month LIBOR plus 0.25 percent. Finally, suppose that six-month LIBOR is almost perfectly correlated with the 26-week T-bill rate and that six-month LIBOR averages 0.5 percent over the 26-week T-bill rate. Given the above, this form of floating-rate financing will cost the firm the 26-week T-bill rate plus 0.75 percent. Including the underwriting costs of the fixed rate note issue and the front-end fees for the interest-rate swap, the all-in cost from this latter financing alternative is determined to be the 26-week T-bill rate plus 1.15 percent.

After comparing the all-in costs of the two alternatives, the corporation in this example chooses the fixed rate note issue coupled with an interest-rate swap.

Forward Rate Agreements

Forward rate agreements (FRAs), also sometimes called future rate agreements, are similar to interest-rate futures but are less standardized and trade over the counter. Unlike futures, FRAs are not guaranteed by a central clearing association. Because FRAs are not highly standarized and are not guaranteed by a central clearing association, they cannot be bought and sold in an anonymous auction market as can futures. A party to an FRA who no longer feels the position is desirable can either hedge the position with a reverse in a second FRA or negotiate a cancellation with the original counterparty. Futures positions, on the other hand, can be closed out by simple offset, without negotiation, at current market prices.

FRAs first appeared in London in 1983.[10] The market expanded rapidly during the second half of 1984 and 1985; and by the end of 1985, monthly trading volume had reached the equivalent of $7

billion (notional principal).[11]   The market for FRAs is primarily an
interbank market dominated by U.S. dollar contracts. London serves
as the main trading center, but New York is rapidly catching up.

FRAs are **cash settlement contracts.** Counterparties most often
use them to hedge interest-rate risk stemming from other transactions. Like swaps, FRAs are off-balance sheet instruments and, hence,
allow the hedging of interest-rate risk without significantly impact-
ing the balance sheet. For the most part, commercial banks take FRA
positions for their own accounts. The contracts can be tailored to the
specific needs of counterparties. Furthermore, because the participants
are well known to one another, performance bonds are not required.
Performance bonds, called margin, are always required of futures
traders.

The rapid growth in the volume of contracts traded led the British Banker's Association, in August of 1985, to develop and publish
a set of recommended terms and conditions for the trading of London interbank FRAs. These terms and conditions have since become
the market standard and, unless otherwise stated, are uniformly used
in FRA dealings in London.

FRAs, like futures, typically have maturities of a year or less, but
they can also be written for much longer periods. It is this ability to
write these contracts for longer periods that makes them potential
substitutes for interest-rate swaps.

At the time an FRA is written, the counterparties select a **reference rate** of interest. The reference rate could be three-month LIBOR,
six-month LIBOR, 26-week T-bill, etc. For purposes of our example,
we will assume the reference rate is three-month LIBOR. Next, the
counterparties agree to a contract rate (a specific value for the reference rate). For example, they might agree to a rate of 8.0 percent for
three-month LIBOR. They also agree to a notional principal. On the
contract's settlement date, the difference between the **prevailing rate**
and the agreed contract rate for the reference rate is determined. This
difference is multiplied by the notional principal and the period of
the deposit to determine the monetary amount due. If the reference
rate on the settlement date is higher than the agreed upon rate, then
the contract purchaser receives payment from the contract seller. If
the reference rate on the settlement date is lower than the agreed
upon rate, then the contract purchaser pays the contract seller.

Forward Exchange Agreements

Forward Exchange Agreements (FXAs) are exchange rate equiva-
lents of FRAs. That is, the counterparties agree to an exchange rate

for the reference foreign exchange rate and a notional principal. The notional principal is stated in terms of a **base currency**. Upon the contract's maturity, the counterparties effect a cash settlement based on the difference between the exchange rate agreed to in the FXA contract and the prevailing exchange rate.

FXAs can be used to hedge foreign-exchange exposure just as FRAs can be used to hedge interest-rate exposure. The market for these contracts is still new and developing. Nevertheless, it is already clear that, within limits, these contracts can be used as substitutes for currency swaps.

Interest-Rate Caps

An **interest-rate cap** is an option-like instrument which is purchased from a rate-cap dealer. Such a dealer makes a market in rate caps—offering to both purchase and sell. The rate-cap contract specifies a reference rate (such as 3-month or 6-month LIBOR), a **strike rate**, a notional principal, and a term. The term typically runs from 1 to 10 years.

The purchaser of a rate cap will receive cash payments from the seller of the rate cap whenever the reference rate exceeds the strike rate. The cash payment is calculated, for a given payment period, as:

$$\text{Cash Payment} = (\text{Ref. Rate - Strike Rate}) \times \text{Not. Prin.} \\ \times \text{Length of Pay. Period}$$

For the rate cap, the cap purchaser will pay the cap seller a single up-front premium calculated as a percentage of the notional principal. For example suppose a premium is quoted as 1.25 percent for a 5-year cap having a strike of 13 percent for the reference rate of six-month LIBOR. If the notional principal were $20 million, the up-front premium payment would be $250,000:

$$\text{Premium} = \$20,000,000 \times 0.0125$$

Rate caps are very useful for setting a limit to the interest rate paid on floating rate liabilities. This type of protection would be of interest to savings and loan associations who are writing rate-capped ARMs (adjustable rate mortgages) and financing them with short-term CDs. The CDs, a source of cost for the thrift, are not capped while the revenue source for the thrift, the mortgages, are capped.

Rate caps are often used in conjunction with swaps to convert one rate type to another and simultaneously cap the floating-rate side.

Interest-Rate Floors

An **interest-rate floor** is very similar to a rate cap except a floor is placed on the interest rate rather than a ceiling. A purchaser of a rate floor would receive payments from the seller whenever the reference rate fell below the strike rate. Again, for this option-like instrument, the purchaser will pay the seller an up-front premium.

Rate floors are useful for depository institutions which issue floating rate liabilities having a guaranteed minimum interest rate (a floor). In these situations, the depository institution has a rate floor on its floating rate liabilities but may not have a floor on its floating rate assets. The purchase of a rate floor allows the depository institution to essentially eliminate the floor on its liabilities.

A couple of side points are in order before we conclude this section. First, rate caps and rate floors are sometimes combined. For example, the user may purchase a rate cap and simultaneously sell a rate floor. The premium received from the rate floor reduces the net cost of the cap. This combination is called a **rate collar**. Second, while FRNs are on-balance sheet instruments, FRAs, FXAs, rate caps, and rate floors are all off-balance sheet instruments. Though these instruments can all be used, to some degree, as substitutes for swaps or as complements to swaps, they are not the principal focus of this book, and we dispense with any further discussion of them.

Summary

Swaps can be used to lower financing costs, hedge interest-rate and exchange-rate exposures, operate on a larger volume in order to exploit economies of scale and gain access to new markets. The intense utilization of the swap product has significantly reduced, through arbitrage, the potential cost-reducing benefits once obtainable with swap finance; but the other uses of swaps remain. Many of the largest firms are only beginning to understand the uses to which they may put swaps, and the use of swaps for these latter purposes continues to expand rapidly.

The uses of swaps discussed in this chapter highlight the versatility of this new financing and risk-management tool. A few of the many other uses of swaps, which have not been discussed in this chapter, include the protection of overseas trading profits by multinationals, and gap management by banks.[12]

Different end-user objectives necessitate different swap variants or combinations of variants. For example, swaps can be written to swap fixed rates into floating rates; to swap zero coupons into floating rates; to swap floating rates into other floating rates; to amortize notional principals; with options to call or put the swap, or to extend the term of the swap; with provisions to delay the commencement of the swap or begin the swap but delay the rate setting; to convert assets rather than liabilities; with rate ceilings and/or rate floors, etc.

There are other financial instruments which can be used, like swaps, to hedge financial risks. These other instruments include futures, options, floating rate notes, forward rate agreements, and forward exchange agreements. The optimal instrument to hedge a given situation will depend on the all-in cost of the different hedging alternatives and the degree of hedging effectiveness associated with each alternative.

Terms

all-in cost
annuity
base currency
basis risk
cash settlement contracts
cost of the hedge
creditworthiness
currency swaps
  amortizing currency swaps
  circus swaps
  fixed-for-fixed rate nonamortizing currency swaps
  fixed-for-floating nonamortizing currency swaps (exchange of
    borrowings)
  floating-for-floating rate nonamortizing currency swaps
economies of scale
end user
financial engineering
floating rate notes (FRNs)
forward exchange agreements (FXAs)

forward rate agreements (FRAs)
interbank market
interest-rate cap
interest-rate floor
interest-rate swaps
  amortizing swaps
  asset-based swaps
  callable swaps
  delayed rate-setting swaps (deferred rate-setting swaps)
  extendable swaps
  fixed-for-floating rate swaps
  floating-for-floating rate swaps (basis swap)
  forward swap (deferred swap)
  mini-max swap
  putable swaps
  rate-capped swaps
  roller-coaster swaps
  zero coupon-for-floating rate swap
negative amortization
prevailing rate
rate collar
reference rate
risk averse firm
strike rate
synthetic instruments

REVIEW QUESTIONS

1. How might interest rate and currency swaps be used by corporations and other commercial entities to reduce financing costs?

2. Using cash-flow diagrams, show how a savings and loan association might use an interest-rate swap to hedge its fixed-rate mortgage portfolio. What special problems does an S&L face in hedging mortgages with swaps, and what special swap provisions might the S&L consequently require?

3. How might hedging allow a depository institution to enhance its profitability?

4. Suppose an automobile company's financing arm borrows short term in the three-month commercial paper market and uses the proceeds so obtained to make four-year fixed-rate automobile loans to the purchaser's of the parent company's automobiles. Describe

the interest-rate risk which this company bears. How might a fixed-for-floating rate swap be used to hedge this risk? To what rate should the floating-rate side of the swap be pegged?

5. What is meant by the "cost of a hedge?" How can this cost be measured?

6. How might hedging exchange-rate risk and interest-rate risk make a firm more creditworthy? How can this benefit the firm?

7. What is a basis swap? Who might use one and how might it be used?

8. Define callable and putable swaps. Who might have use for these types of swaps?

9. What is a rate-capped swap, and who might have a use for this type of swap?

10. How might a fixed-for-fixed currency swap be created from a fixed-for-floating currency swap and a fixed-for-floating interest rate swap? Illustrate by means of cash-flow diagrams.

ENDNOTES

1. The end user of the swap need not be, and often is not, a for-profit commercial firm. Many swaps have been arranged to provide reduced-cost financing for sovereign nations and international organizations. The Kingdom of Sweden is a leading user of swap finance and thus an example of the former (see Grant 1985). The World Bank, discussed in Chapter 1, is a leading user and excellent example of the latter, see Wallich (1984).

2. An **annuity** is a series of equal-sized payments spread out at equal intervals in time. They are valued with the aid of present value annuity arithmetic.

3. This sum is determined with the aid of present value arithmetic. In particular, 60 quarterly payments of DM 3,235,340 have a present value of DM 100 million at an annual discount rate (interest rate) of 10 percent (compounded quarterly). Each payment represents interest and a partial repayment of principal.

4. The assumption that the current spot exchange rate of deutsche marks for dollars is an unbiased estimate of all future spot exchange rates of deutsche marks for dollars is made for simplicity of illustration only. In fact, the current spot exchange rate of one currency for another will generally not be an unbiased

estimate of the future spot exchange rates for those two currencies. In efficient capital and currency markets, the relationship between these forward exchange rates and the respective countries nominal interest rates is explained by the interest-rate parity theorem. The interested reader should see Marshall (1989, chapter 11).

5. For a detailed discussion of the behavior of the firm hedging in futures in the presence of positive hedging costs, see Marshall (1989, chapter 7). The arguments presented there are directly extendable to a swap hedge.

6. For a very nice discussion of the many areas encompassed by financial engineering, see Finnerty (1988).

7. Most often, this "formula" simply specifies the spread over Treasury which will be used to fix the rate at the time the swap coupon is set.

8. Rate-capped swaps are not the only means by which rate-capped mortgages can be hedged. Other instruments useful for this purpose include futures, options, and rated-capped floating rate notes. Floating rate notes and rate caps are discussed later in this chapter.

9. The first documented public offering of FRNs in the U.S. is attributed to Mortgage Investors of Washington which offered, on 1 November 1973, $15 million of Floating Rate (eight percent to twelve percent) Senior Subordinated Notes due 1 November 1980. For a more detailed discussion of the history of the floating-rate debt market, see Wilson (1987). For a discussion of the role of FRNs in financial engineering, see Smith (1989).

10. See British Bankers' Association (1985).

11. See Bank for International Settlements (1986).

12. For a discussion of the use of swaps and related instruments to protect overseas trading profits, see Lota-Gerd (1985). For a discussion of the use of swaps in gap management by banks and other depository institutions, see Wade (1987), and Brown and Smith (1989).

REFERENCES AND SUGGESTED READING

Bank for International Settlements, *Recent Innovations in International Banking* (1986).

Bicksler, J. and A. H. Chen. "An Economic Analysis of Interest Rate Swaps." *Journal of Finance*, 41:3, 645-655 (July 1986).

British Bankers' Association. *Forward Rate Agreements: FRABBA Terms* (1985).

Brown, K.C. and D.J. Smith. "Recent Innovations in Interest-Rate Risk Management and the Reintermediation of Commercial Bank Lending." *Financial Management*, vol. 17 (4) (Winter 1988).

Finnerty, J.D. "Financial Engineering in Corporate Finance: An Overview." *Financial Management*, vol. 17 (4) (Winter 1988).

Gelardin, J. "A Complex Market for Floating Rate Notes." *Euromoney*, 17-19 (January 1986).

Grant, C. "Swedish Lessons for the French." *Euromoney*, 107-114 (January 1985).

Hume, J. G. "Remaining Calm in Troubled Markets: The Growth of Risk Hedging Vehicles." *Journal of Commercial Bank Lending*, 7:7 36-44 (December 1984).

Loeys, J. "Interest Rate Swaps: A New Tool for Managing Risk." *Business Review* (Federal Reserve Bank of Philadelphia) (May/June 1985).

Lota-Gerd, P. E. "Forward Foreign Exchange: Protecting Overseas Trading Profits." *Credit and Financial Management*, 87:5, 31-38 (June 1985).

Madura, J. and C. Williams "Hedging Mortgages with Interest Rate Swaps vs Caps: How to Choose." *Real Estate Finance Journal*, 3:1, 90-96 (Summer 1987).

Mahajan, A. and D. Mehta. "Strong Form Efficiency of the Foreign Exchange Market and Bank Positions." *Journal of Financial Research*, 7:3, 197-207 (Fall 1984).

Marshall, J. F. *Futures and Option Contracting: Theory and Practice* (Cincinnati: South-Western Publishing Co., 1989).

Simonson, D. G. "Asset/Liability: A Time for Swaps." *United States Banker*, 98:2, 51052 (February 1987).

Smith, C. W., C. W. Smithson, and L.W. Wakeman. "The Market for Interest Rate Swaps." *Financial Management*, vol. 17 (4) (Winter 1988).

Smith, D. J., "The Pricing of Bull and Bear Floating Rate Notes: An Application of Financial Engineering." *Financial Management*, vol. 17 (4) (Winter 1988).

Wade, R. E. "Managing a Negative Gap in a Rising Interest Rate Environment," *Financial Managers' Statement*, 9:4, 33-37 (July 1987).

Wallich, C. I. "The World Bank's Currency Swaps." *Finance and Development*, 2:1, 15-19 (June 1984).

Wilson, R. S. "Domestic Floating-Rate and Adjustable-Rate Debt Securities." In *Handbook of Fixed Income Securities*, F. J. Fabozzi and I. M. Pollack, eds., 2d ed., (Homewood, IL: Dow Jones-Irwin, 1987).

CHAPTER 3

THE PRICING OF SWAPS

Overview

In this chapter, we consider how swap banks price swaps. We assume that the swap bank is acting as a dealer in swaps and, hence, as a counterparty to the swap rather than as a swap broker. The pricing of the swap is important for both the swap bank and the corporate user. The corporate user might want to compare the pricing of swaps offered by several swap banks and compare the all-in cost of these swap alternatives to the all-in cost of other financing and/or other risk-management opportunities available.

The bank's pricing will hinge on a number of things. These include (1) the maturity of the swap, (2) the structure of the swap, (3) the availability of other counterparties with whom the bank can offset the swap, (4) the creditworthiness of the client counterparty, (5) the demand and supply conditions for credit generally and for swaps in particular in all countries whose currencies are involved in the swap, and (6) any regulatory constraints on the flow of capital that impact on the efficiency of the markets.

We begin with an examination of the pricing of interest-rate swaps. We start with the plain vanilla fixed-for-floating rate swap based on bullet transactions. We then complicate the analysis slightly by introducing amortization and payment frequency considerations. We assume the swap bank offsets its swaps in the U.S. Treasury and/or Eurodollar markets until such time as it can offset the swaps with other counterparties. After completing our look at the pricing of interest-rate swaps, we consider the pricing of currency swaps. We begin with the plain vanilla currency swap which, as mentioned in Chapter 2, is called an exchange of borrowings. We then consider amortizing currency swaps and pricing complications introduced by off-market transactions. Finally, we consider the pricing of fixed-for-fixed rate currency swaps created through a combination of a fixed-for-floating interest-rate swap and fixed-for-floating exchange of borrowings (currency swap).

One important point is in order before we begin. In the discussion of swap pricing which follows, we employ bid-asked spreads which range to 25 basis points. Such swap spreads were typical in swap bank pricing in the mid-1980s, but they have narrowed considerably during the last few years. Spreads of 10 basis points or less are more realistic today. In any case, the actual size of the spread is not very important to understanding the theory involved.

Indication Pricing Schedules: The Interest-Rate Swap

Swap banks regularly prepare **indication pricing schedules** for use by their capital market personnel. These schedules are updated frequently to take account of changing market conditions. An indication pricing schedule provides the swap dealer with guidelines for pricing swaps. Prices take the form of interest rates and are stated in terms of basis points (bps). Each basis point is 1/100th of one percent. In the case of dollar-based interest rates, the fixed-rate side of the swap is usually stated as a spread over prevailing yields on "**on the runs**" U.S. Treasury securities. On the runs are the securities of a given maturity which were most recently auctioned. For example, five years ago the Treasury auctioned 10-year notes. With the passage of time, these 10-year notes have become 5-year notes. If the Treasury now auctions a new issue of 5-year notes, there are then at least two 5-year T-note issues simultaneously trading. The most recent issues (the on the runs) have the more current coupon and tend to be more liquid than the older issues. The floating-rate side is most often taken to be LIBOR flat. The pricing structure assumes bullet transactions. That is, as with Treasury securities, it is assumed that the principal is repaid in a lump sum at maturity. A minor complication introduced by this pricing scheme is that the interest rate on the fixed-rate side of a swap is quoted as a semiannual **bond equivalent yield**. Bond equivalent yields are based on a 365-day year. The floating-rate side is usually tied to LIBOR. LIBOR is quoted as a **money market yield**. Money market yields are based on a 360-day year. This difference in yield conventions often necessitates some conversions to make the rates more directly comparable. We address this issue shortly.

In the early days of swaps, it was quite common for the swap bank to require a **front-end fee** for arranging the swap. The front-end fee was negotiable and could run as much as 1/2 of a percentage point. The justification for the front-end fee was the time it took to write the swap documentation and the time it took to work with the client to design a swap that would accomplish the client's objectives. With the increasing standardization of swaps, front-end fees have all but disappeared. Today, a front-end fee will only be imposed in those cases in which some fancy financial engineering is required or in which the client is purchasing some special option-like feature. Front-end fees have never been common on interbank swaps.[1]

Consider a typical indication pricing schedule for swaps having various maturities as depicted in Exhibit 3.1. The prices indicated are for fixed-for-floating interest-rate swaps and assume semiannual compounding (sa). Although we always state interest rates on an annual basis, it is customary to call an annual rate of interest compounded semiannually a **semiannual rate**. For example, the phrase "a semiannual rate of 8 percent" means an annual interest rate of 8 percent compounded semiannually. The phrase "an annual rate of 8 percent" means an annual interest rate of 8 percent compounded annually.

EXHIBIT 3.1

INDICATION PRICING FOR INTEREST-RATE SWAPS

Maturity	Bank Pays Fixed Rate	Bank Receives Fixed Rate	Current TN Rate
2 years	2 yr TN sa + 20 bps	2 yr TN sa + 45 bps	8.55 percent
3 years	3 yr TN sa + 25 bps	3 yr TN sa + 52 bps	8.72 percent
4 years	4 yr TN sa + 28 bps	4 yr TN sa + 58 bps	8.85 percent
5 years	5 yr TN sa + 34 bps	5 yr TN sa + 60 bps	8.92 percent
6 years	6 yr TN sa + 38 bps	6 yr TN sa + 66 bps	8.96 percent
7 years	7 yr TN sa + 40 bps	7 yr TN sa + 70 bps	9.00 percent
10 years	10 yr TN sa + 50 bps	10 yr TN sa + 84 bps	9.08 percent

N.B. The schedule assumes semiannual rates and bullet transactions. TN denotes the Treasury Note rate.

Let's consider a simple example: A corporation has determined that it can sell $25 million of 5-year nonamortizing debt at par by offering a semiannual coupon of 9.675 percent.[2] It prefers floating-rate liabilities to fixed-rate liabilities and approaches the capital markets group of our swap bank to arrange an interest-rate swap. Call this corporate client counterparty number 1.

The swap bank has been asked to pay fixed rate and receive floating rate. Since the bank has been asked to pay fixed rate, the bank offers to pay 9.26 percent (5-year TN rate + 34 bps) in exchange for six-month LIBOR flat. The corporate client's net cost of funds, after the interest-rate swap, appears to be LIBOR + 0.415 percent (9.675% + LIBOR - 9.260%). This is not, however, quite correct. Because the fixed-rate sides are bond equivalent yields, the difference between them, 0.415 percent, is also a bond equivalent. This difference cannot be added directly to LIBOR without first converting it to a money market yield equivalent. Remember, 6-M LIBOR is quoted as a semiannual money market yield (MMY) and based on the assumption of a 360-day year, while the fixed-rate side of a fixed-for-floating rate swap is quoted as a semiannual bond equivalent yield (BEY) and based on the assumption of a 365-day year.

To combine these values correctly, we must transform the fixed-rate differential, 0.415 percent, to its money market yield equivalent. The conversion formula appears as Equation 3.1.[3] This conversion is simple because both 6-M LIBOR and the swap coupon are semiannual rates. When the payment frequencies are mismatched (annual vs. semiannual, for example) the conversions are somewhat more complex.

EQUATION 3.1

$$MMY \text{ differential} = BEY \text{ differential} \times \frac{360}{365}$$

$$= 0.415 \text{ percent} \times \frac{360}{365}$$

$$= 0.409 \text{ percent}$$

The final floating-rate cost of funding for this corporate client is then LIBOR + 0.409 percent. The cash flows associated with this swap are depicted in Exhibit 3.2. As it happens, had this corporate client borrowed directly in the floating-rate market, it would have been required to pay LIBOR plus 1.25 percent.

EXHIBIT 3.2

CASH FLOWS BETWEEN COUNTERPARTY 1 AND SWAP BANK

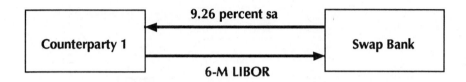

($25 million notional principal)

The swap bank above would look for an opportunity to offset this swap with another swap. Until it can do so, however, the bank will hedge in T-notes and Eurodollars (or T-bills). For example, since the swap bank has agreed to pay fixed rate and receive floating rate, it might short $25 million (market value) six-month Treasury bills and use the proceeds from this sale to purchase $25 million (market value) of 5-year Treasury notes.[4] The bank can obtain the securities for the short sale by a **reverse repurchase agreement** (reverse) with another institution. In a reverse, the bank "purchases" a security from another party and agrees to "sell" the security back to this same party at a specific later date for a specific price. Alternatively, the swap bank may hold a portfolio of Treasury securities separate and distinct from its swap operations. For example, the portfolio might represent an investment portfolio that the bank manages either for itself or for its clients, or the swap bank might be a market maker in Treasuries (government securities dealer). These portfolios can serve as the source of the securities which the swap bank sells short. The swap desk will pay other departments of the bank for these securities. The cost of these intrabank borrowings is called the **transfer pricing rate** (TPR). The transaction may be viewed as equivalent to a reverse repurchase agreement between departments within the bank. For purposes of this text, we assume that the TPR is the T-bill rate. In practice, the TPR will usually be at a premium to Treasuries. The cash flows for the swap bank are depicted in Exhibit 3.3.

The swap bank prefers to offset the swaps to which it is a counterparty with matching swaps with other counterparties. The Treasury/ Eurodollar positions represent hedges placed only until such time as

EXHIBIT 3.3

CASH FLOWS AFTER OFFSET
IN GOVERNMENT SECURITIES MARKET

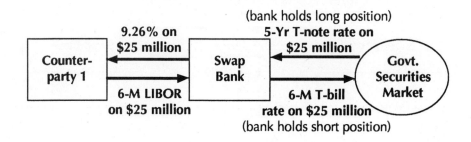

a matched swap can be arranged. Importantly, if the swap bank hedges in T-bills, as opposed to Eurodollars, it will have a residual basis risk as LIBOR and the T-bill rate are not perfectly correlated. We address this point more fully in the next chapter.

Suppose now that another corporate client approaches the swap bank in need of $30 million of fixed-rate dollar financing. This firm has a comparative advantage in the floating-rate (LIBOR) market. It can sell semiannual 5-year nonamortizing floating rate notes (FRNs) at par by paying six-month LIBOR plus 150 bps. Through the vehicle of the swap, the corporate client would like to convert this floating-rate liability into a fixed-rate liability. The swap bank is asked to receive fixed rate and pay floating rate. Call this corporate client counterparty number 2.

The swap bank has been asked to receive fixed rate and pay floating rate. We will assume that the indication pricing schedule depicted in Exhibit 3.1 is still in effect. Since the bank has been asked to receive fixed rate, it would require that counterparty 2 pay 9.52 percent (5-year TN rate + 60 bps) in exchange for the bank paying six-month LIBOR flat. To calculate counterparty 2's net cost of funds, we must first convert the floating-rate spread over LIBOR (1.5 percent), which is stated on a money market yield basis, to a bond equivalent yield basis. Equation 3.1 allowed us to move from a bond equivalent yield to money market yield; however, in this case, we need to move in the opposite direction. Equation 3.2 allows us to move from a money market yield to a bond equivalent yield. Again, this conversion is simple because both rates are already stated on a semiannual basis. If the payment frequencies were mismatched, the conversions would be more complex.

EQUATION 3.2

$$BEY \text{ differential} = MMY \text{ differential} \times \frac{365}{360}$$

$$= 1.5 \text{ percent} \times \frac{365}{360}$$

$$= 1.521 \text{ percent}$$

The conversion yields the value 1.521 percent. Counterparty 2's net cost of funds, after the interest-rate swap, is then 11.041 percent (LIBOR + 1.521 percent - LIBOR + 9.52 percent). As it happens, this firm could have borrowed fixed-rate funds directly at a cost of 11.375 percent.

The cash flows between the bank and counterparty 2 are depicted in Exhibit 3.4. The swap bank could offset its position with counterparty 2 by selling $30 million (market value) of 5-year Treasury notes short and by using the proceeds from this short sale to purchase $30 million (market value) of six-month T-bills.

EXHIBIT 3.4

CASH FLOWS BETWEEN COUNTERPARTY 2 AND SWAP BANK

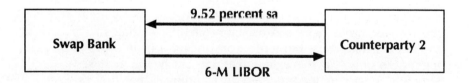

($30 million notional principal)

Notice that the bank's cash flows with counterparty 2 are very nearly the mirror image of the bank's cash flows with counterparty 1. In fact, if the swap bank lifts its positions in the Treasury market which it is using to hedge its swap with counterparty 1, it will only require a $5 million position in Treasuries/Eurodollars to hedge the interest-rate exposure stemming from its swap with counterparty 2. The flows, from the swap bank's perspective, are depicted in Exhibit 3.5.

EXHIBIT 3.5

CASH FLOWS BETWEEN COUNTERPARTIES AND SWAP BANK WITH RESIDUAL POSITION IN GOVERNMENT SECURITIES

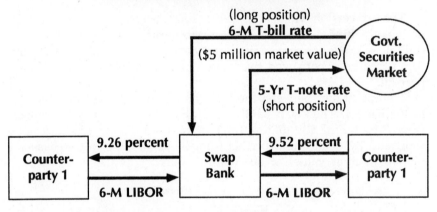

The indication pricing schedule used to price the swaps made between the swap bank and counterparties 1 and 2 assumes that the swaps are of the plain vanilla fixed-for-floating rate variety and that the counterparties have a satisfactory credit standing in the eyes of the swap bank. Thus, the indication pricing schedule provides starting prices only. To the extent that the swap will require a special structure, or a counterparty's credit standing is not first rate, or the swap exposes the bank to special risks, the swap pricing will have to be adjusted to reflect these factors. Price adjustments might take the form of a wider swap bid-asked spread or a front-end fee or both. However, as discussed earlier, front-end fees are no longer typical except when special financial engineering is required or when the swap incorporates an option-like feature. In the latter case, the front-end fees are best viewed as option premiums.

For example, if counterparty 1, who is paying the equivalent of LIBOR plus 0.409 percent, desired a rate cap of 12.5 percent, the swap bank would likely oblige; but it would add a front-end fee and/or raise the floating-rate payment. Suppose this particular swap bank will oblige counterparty 1's request for a rate cap, but it will require a front-end fee of 1/4 point (25 basis points) and increase the counterparty's rate to LIBOR plus 0.550 percent. Similar fees and adjustments would be made if the counterparty required a call feature, a put feature, a rate floor, and so on.

Adjustments To Indication Pricing

The indication pricing schedule assumes that payments are to be made semiannually and that all transactions are bullet transactions. It is not unusual for one or both of these assumptions to fail. When they do fail, an adjustment in pricing must be made.

We will consider first the pricing adjustments necessitated by a failure of the nonamortizing bullet-transaction assumption. Following this, we consider the adjustments necessitated by a failure of the semiannual payment assumption.

Amortizing Loans: Duration Versus Average Life

The indication pricing schedule assumes that the swap is nonamortizing so that the interest payments are calculated on the same notional principal throughout the term of the swap. Suppose instead that the swap bank's client requires a swap based upon amortizing principal. Any number of amortizing schedules are possible. For example, the client might require that the notional principal underlying the swap be reduced by a fixed dollar amount each year (often called a **sinking fund** schedule); or, the client might require that the notional principal be reduced by a fixed dollar amount each year beginning after some defined **grace period** during which no amortization of notional principal occurs; or, the client might wish to amortize the principal at an increasing rate as is customary with mortgage-type amortization schedules (perhaps the client is a savings and loan looking to hedge the interest-rate risk associated with its mortgage portfolio).

As already argued, most swap banks price the fixed-rate side of an interest-rate swap as a spread over Treasury securities. Treasury debt is always nonamortizing. That is, the Treasury pays periodic (semiannual) interest but does not repay any principal on a Treasury note or bond until such time as the note or bond matures. At maturity, the Treasury repays all principal in a single transaction. Given the nonamortizing nature of Treasury securities, it is not appropriate to base the price of an N-year amortizing swap on the prevailing yield of an N-year nonamortizing Treasury security.

Operatives in the debt markets, including commercial banks, investment banks, government securities dealers, etc., know that, all other things being equal, the longer the maturity associated with a given debt instrument, the more price sensitive will the debt instrument be to fluctuations in yield levels. It is partly for this reason that long-term debt instruments are regarded as more risky than are short-term debt instruments. This fact forms the foundation for one well-known, though not universally accepted, explanation for the shape of the Treasury **yield curve**—the liquidity preference theory—which holds that the yield on a debt instrument is directly related to its price sensitivity to interest-rate fluctuations.[5] However, it has also long been known that maturity alone is not the sole determinant of a debt instrument's price sensitivity to changes in interest rates. A second, and very important determinant is the speed with which the debt principal amortizes. Other, lesser important, factors include the size of the coupon payments, the frequency of the coupon payments, and the yield presently afforded by the instrument.

In 1938, Frederick Macaulay developed a measure of price sensitivity to yield changes that incorporates all five of the factors which influence price sensitivity.[6] This measure is known as **duration**. Assuming equal basis point changes in yield, two debt instruments having identical durations will have identical interest-rate sensitivities. Further, the ratio of two debt instruments' durations is an accurate measure of their relative price sensitivities to equivalent yield changes when such price sensitivity is stated on a percentage basis. Duration, which is measured in years and denoted here by D, is a weighted-average time to the maturity of the instrument. The weights are the ratios of the present values of the future cash flows (including both interest and principal) to the current market price of the instrument. The current price of the instrument is, of course, the sum of the present value of all future cash flows associated with the instrument. That is,

EQUATION 3.3

$$D = \sum_{t}^{m \cdot T} w_t \cdot (t/m)$$

$$\text{where } w_t = \frac{CF(t/m) \cdot (1 + y/m)^{-t}}{\sum_t CF(t/m) \cdot (1 + y/m)^{-t}} \qquad\qquad t = 1,2,3,\ldots m \cdot T$$

$CF(t/m)$: Cash flow at time t/m (time measured in years).
     y: Present yield on instrument.
    m: The number of payment periods per year.

Because of its long-standing role as a measure of a debt instrument's price sensitivity to fluctuation's in yield (interest-rate risk), it seems logical to use duration in the pricing of the fixed-rate side of interest-rate and currency swaps.[7] Unfortunately, duration has proven unsatisfactory for this purpose. The duration equation allows one to determine an instrument's duration if one knows its yield. The problem is, we don't know the instrument's duration *and* we don't know the appropriate yield—which is the fixed rate of interest used for the swap coupon. This is, after all, what we are trying to determine.

The solution to pricing the fixed-rate side of the swap is to use a weighted-average measure of the times at which notional principal is amortized where the weights are formed without reference to yield. **Average life** is such a measure.[8]

The average life of an instrument is found by forming the product of the principal repayment and the time at which that principal repayment will be made. These products are then summed, and the sum is divided by the notional principal at the start of the swap. It is important to remember that in interest-rate swaps these principal repayments are only notional. The notional nature of the principal, however, does not affect the calculation of the average life.

EQUATION 3.4

$$AL = \frac{\sum P(t) \cdot t}{IP}$$

  AL: average life
$P(t)$: principal repaid (or cancelled) at time t
  IP: initial principal (principal at start of swap)

Let's consider a simple example: Suppose a firm required an amortizing swap having an initial notional principal of $9.5 million and a term of 9.5 years with semiannual payments. The principal will amortize under a semiannual sinking-fund type schedule with

notional principal payments of $0.5 million each.[9] Thus, the first
payment is due at time 0.5, the second is due at time 1.0, and so on
until the last, that is due at time 9.5. The first product is formed by
multiplying $0.5 million by 0.5; the second is formed by multiplying
$0.5 million by 1; and so on.

These products are then summed to get 47.5 million. Finally, this
sum is divided by the initial notional principal of 9.5 million to get
an average life of 5 years. Thus, the swap has an average life of 5
years. The calculation of this average life is repeated below.

Time		Principal Repaid		Product
0.5	x	$0.5 M	=	$0.25 M
1.0	x	$0.5 M	=	$0.50 M
.	.	.	.	.
.	.	.	.	.
.	.	.	.	.
9.5	x	$0.5 M	=	$4.75 M
			Sum	47.50 M

AL = 47.5 ÷ 9.5 = 5 years

Once the average life has been determined, we simply treat the
swap as though it is equivalent to a T-note having a maturity equal
to the swap's average life. We then look to the indication pricing
schedule for the pricing of swaps of this term. This particular swap
would then be priced from the 5-year T-note. The average life of a
nonamortizing instrument, such as a T-note, is identical to its term
to maturity.

Suppose the five-year T-note is currently yielding 8.75 percent.
Using the duration formula, we find that the five-year T-note has a
duration of 3.98. Using the same yield to calculate the duration of
the amortizing swap, we find that the swap has a duration of 3.93.
Thus, the duration of the swap and the duration of the T-note having the same average life are nearly the same—although not necessarily identical.

An important argument in favor of the use of average life, as
opposed to duration, in the pricing of swaps lies in the treatment of
interest. On a typical debt instrument, interest payments flow only
one way. In a swap, interest payments flow two ways and are therefore largely offsetting. The offsetting nature of the interest payments
suggests a strong argument for focusing on the principal alone—which
is precisely what average life does.

One final point is in order on selecting the appropriate instrument on which to price a swap. With the widespread stripping of coupon-bearing Treasury securities to create zero-coupon Treasury products, sufficient liquidity has developed in zero-coupon Treasuries for the emergence of a well-defined zero-coupon yield curve. The **zero-coupon yield curve** depicts the relationship between the yields on zero-coupon Treasuries and their respective maturities. Zero-coupon securities have the unique property that their duration, average life, and maturity are identical.

At present, many swap banks use the zero-coupon yield curve as the basis of their swap hedging operations but continue to price their swap products off the conventional yield curve. It is likely, that, in time, swap banks may switch to pricing their swap products off the zero-coupon yield curve. In keeping with common practice, however, we will continue to use the regular coupon bearing Treasury securities for our pricing discussion.

Semiannual Rates Versus Other Payment Frequencies

Interest-rate swaps priced as a **spread over Treasuries** assume semiannual interest payments. When the bank's client requires annual payments, as opposed to semiannual payments, the bank must adjust the fixed rate of interest to reflect this difference.

Consider again the case of counterparty 2 which had approached the swap bank for a 5-year fixed-for-floating interest-rate swap. This party would pay fixed rate and receive floating rate. The bank quotes a semiannual fixed rate of 9.52 percent (5-year TN + 60 bps). Counterparty 2 now indicates that it prefers annual fixed-rate payments although it still wishes to receive semiannual floating-rate payments based on six-month LIBOR.

The swap bank is agreeable but must now determine the annual rate which is equivalent to a semiannual rate of 9.52 percent. The procedure for determining the equivalent annual rate is founded on basic time-value arithmetic. That is, we calculate the annual interest rate which would provide the same future value, for a given starting sum, as would the semiannual rate. This calculation is as follows:

$$r_{an} = (1 + r_{sa}/2)^2 - 1$$

where r_{an} denotes the annual interest rate and r_{sa} denotes the semiannual interest rate. More generally, we can convert an interest rate stated on one payment frequency into an interest rate stated on another payment frequency using the relationship given by Equation 3.5.

EQUATION 3.5

$$r_m = m \cdot [(1 + \frac{r_z}{z})^{z/m} - 1]$$

r_m: Annual rate of interest assuming m compoundings per year.
r_z: Annual rate of interest assuming z compoundings per year.

In this more general formulation, m would be 1 if the rate r_m were annual; z would be 2 if the rate r_z were semiannual; and so on. These conversions ignore the issue of reinvestment risk. **Reinvestment risk** is the risk that income received from an investment will be reinvested at a rate which differs from the rate which prevailed at the time the investment was acquired. The swap bank might be expected to attach a premium to its swap pricing when the swap structure gives rise to reinvestment risk. This risk, however, is small in comparison to other risks which we will discuss shortly, and so we will ignore it.

Consider again the swap bank's situation with respect to counterparty 2. Counterparty 2 requires a payment schedule that provides for annual rather than semiannual payments of fixed-rate interest. The bank calculates the annual interest rate using Equation 3.5.

$$r_1 = 1 \cdot [(1 + .0952/2)^{2/1} - 1] = 9.747\%$$

The swap bank now offers its client a fixed-for-floating rate swap in which the bank would pay semiannual interest to the client at the rate of six-month LIBOR in exchange for the client's annual payments to the bank at the rate of 9.747 percent.

There is one additional problem with this swap from the swap bank's perspective. Since the bank pays the client semiannually, but the client only pays the bank annually; there is a payment mismatch which exposes the bank to considerable credit risk. For example, suppose that the floating-rate side is initially set at 8.5 percent and that six months after the swap documents are executed the bank pays its counterparty client $1.275 million [1/2 of 8.5 percent on $30 million]. Next, suppose that, six months later, the counterparty client defaults at the time the counterparty is due to make its first payment to the bank. While the counterparty's default frees the bank from its obligation to make the current and future interest payments, as per the rights of set-off contained in the terms and conditions of the swap agreement, the bank has already made its first payment to the counterparty. It must now utilize the swap's default provisions to try to recover its losses.

This example illustrates the extra level of risk associated with entering swaps having payment timing mismatches. We will consider this problem again, and the steps the swap bank might take to alleviate it, in Chapter 4. One final point is, however, in order. Because payment timing mismatches increase the risk exposure of the swap bank, we might expect that the swap bank will insist on additional compensation from its counterparty client. For example, the bank might add a few basis points to the fixed rate its counterparty client is required to pay.

It is important to note that there is almost always some credit risk to the swap bank from its swap activities. While the rights of set-off relieve the swap bank from making payments to its counterparty should the counterparty default, the default does not relieve the swap bank of its commitments to other counterparties—including those with whom the bank has matched the defaulted swap. Thus, credit risk is very real even when the timing of the payments are perfectly matched. Clearly, however, mismatched timing of payments amplifies credit risk.

Market Imbalances and Pay/Receive Rate Adjustments

The difference between the fixed rate a swap bank must receive and the fixed rate it is willing to pay at any given average life is its bid-asked spread for swaps having that average life. In preparing its indication pricing schedules and implied spreads, the swap bank must take several things into consideration. Of major importance, of course, are the competitive pressures of the market. The swap bank must offer competitive swap pricing if it is to attract rate-conscious corporate clients.

Suppose that the swap bank using the indication pricing schedule appearing in Exhibit 3.1 finds that it is attracting considerable 5-year average life fixed-for-floating swap activity on the bank-pays-fixed-rate side but very little swap activity on the other side. The swap bank prefers to offset its swaps with other swaps rather than resorting to hedging in the cash market for Treasury securities. Looking again at the bank's current pricing for 5-year average life swaps, we can see that the bank needs to attract additional swap activity on the bank-receives-fixed-rate side. At present, the bank's base pricing requires TN + 60 bps from fixed-rate payers. The bank can attract additional activity on the bank-receives-fixed-rate side by lowering the fixed rate it requires of fixed-rate paying counterparties. For example, it might lower its price on 5-year average life swaps to TN + 58 bps. At the same time, it might lower the rate that it will pay so as to discourage new swaps on the bank-pays-fixed-rate side until such time as it can fully offset its existing portfolio of swaps. For example, it might lower its bank-pays rate to TN + 31 bps.

	Maturity	Bank Pays Fixed-Rate	Bank Receives Fixed-Rate	Current TN Rate
old	5 years	5 yr TN sa + 34 bps	5 yr TN sa + 60 bps	8.92 percent
new	5 years	5 yr TN sa + 31 bps	5 yr TN sa + 58 bps	8.92 percent

By frequently adjusting its pay/receive rates, the swap bank is able to attract additional counterparties on the side of the market it prefers and to thereby correct market imbalances. In more extreme cases, the swap bank might find that some of the counterparties attracted to its prevailing rate are themselves swap banks who have developed imbalances on the other side of the fixed-for-floating rate market.

Indication Pricing Schedules: Currency Swaps

In the plain vanilla currency swap, the counterparty client looks to swap a fixed-rate obligation in one currency for a floating-rate obligation in another currency. By using a currency swap in conjunction with an interest-rate swap, we can convert a fixed-rate obligation in one currency to a fixed-rate obligation in another currency; or, alternatively, we can use a currency swap in conjunction with an interest-rate swap to convert a floating-rate obligation in one currency to a floating-rate obligation in another currency.

In this section, we concentrate on the pricing of fixed-for-floating rate currency swaps. The swap bank's international capital markets team will estimate appropriate pay and receive fixed rates for all of the currencies in which the bank makes a market. All rates are against six-month LIBOR flat. The fixed rates may be stated on an annual or a semiannual basis, and the adjustment from annual to semiannual or vice versa is exactly the same as that described in our discussion of rate adjustments for interest-rate swaps. So we do not discuss it further. Instead, we will assume that the rates are all stated on a semiannual basis.

In the case of currency swaps, indication pricings are often stated as a midrate to which some number of basis points is added or subtracted depending on whether the swap bank is to receive or pay fixed rate. Such a schedule is depicted for deutsche mark-to-dollar rates in Exhibit 3.6.

EXHIBIT 3.6

INDICATION PRICING FOR
DEUTSCHE MARK/DOLLAR SWAPS

Maturity	Midrate
2 years	6.25% sa
3 years	6.48% sa
4 years	6.65% sa
5 years	6.78% sa
6 years	6.88% sa
7 years	6.96% sa
10 years	7.10% sa

N.B. The rates above are midrates. To these rates, deduct 1/8 percent (12.5 bps) if the bank is paying fixed rate. Add 1/8 percent (12.5 bps) if the bank is receiving fixed rate. All principal transactions are assumed to be bullet transactions.

The structure of the DM/US indication pricing in Exhibit 3.6 is typical of currency swaps, although the size of the bid-asked spread (25 bps) is excessive by current standards. The swap bank would likely offer similar schedules for the other major hard currencies including the Swiss franc, French franc, British pound, Canadian dollar, and Japanese yen.

As already mentioned, the rates in Exhibit 3.6 are midrates. The actual pay/receive rates are found by deducting/adding the appropriate premium to the midrate. For the straight U.S. dollar interest-rate swaps, the indication pricing schedule depicted in Exhibit 3.1 lists both the bank's pay and receive rates. Nevertheless, we can obtain a midrate for interest-rate swaps by simply taking the average of the pay and receive rates. For example, for the 5-year interest-rate swap the midrate is 9.39 percent [(9.26 + 9.52)   2].

Consider now a simple example: A German firm approaches our swap bank looking to convert a DM 35 million 5-year semiannual fixed-rate liability into a floating-rate dollar liability. The swap bank offers an exchange of borrowings (straight currency swap) at the current spot exchange rate of 1.75 DM/US. At the current exchange rate, the principal is $20 million. Since the bank will be paying fixed rate, the rate is found by taking the 5-year midrate and deducting 1/8 percent. This calculation produces a rate of 6.655 percent (6.78 - 0.125). Thus, the German counterparty client would pay the swap bank six-month LIBOR on principal of $20 million, and the swap bank would pay the German firm 6.655 percent sa on DM 35 million.

Unlike an interest-rate swap, in which there is no exchange of principals, there often is an exchange of principals in the straight currency swap. That is, at the commencement of the swap, the German firm would exchange its DM 35 million for the bank's $20 million. For the next five years, the two parties would pay each other interest at the rates indicated. After five years, the two parties would reexchange principals at the same exchange rate used for the initial exchange of principals, i.e., 1.75 DM/US. The straight currency swap clearly involves three separate cash flows: (1) initial exchange of principals; (2) interest payments; and (3) reexchange of principals. These are depicted in Exhibits 3.7, 3.8, and 3.9.

As with the interest-rate swap, the swap bank makes its profit from its bid-asked spread. For this swap bank, the spread is currently 1/4 point (25 bps) because the bank is adding and subtracting 1/8 from its midrate. The bank is, of course, looking to offset its exchange-rate and interest-rate exposures. These exposures are most easily offset by finding another counterparty client with matching

EXHIBIT 3.7

CURRENCY SWAP (EXCHANGE OF BORROWINGS) INITIAL EXCHANGE OF PRINCIPALS

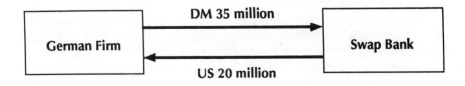

EXHIBIT 3.8

CURRENCY SWAP (EXCHANGE OF BORROWINGS) CASH FLOWS BETWEEN EXCHANGES OF PRINCIPALS

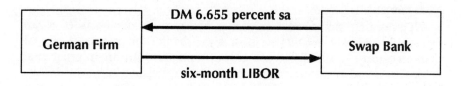

EXHIBIT 3.9

CURRENCY SWAP (EXCHANGE OF BORROWINGS) REEXCHANGE OF PRINCIPALS

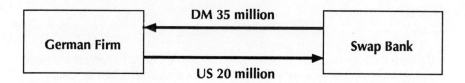

needs. Such a client would be looking to exchange 20 million 5-year floating-rate dollars for fixed-rate deutsche marks. Assuming the bank has such a client immediately available, the bank would offer to swap the currencies at the current spot exchange rate of 1.75 DM/US. The bank would pay this second counterparty six-month LIBOR flat in exchange for the second counterparty client paying the bank DM 6.905 percent sa.

By offsetting the currency and interest exchanges with a second counterparty having cash flow needs that match those of the first, the bank is fully hedged against fluctuations in both exchange rates and interest rates. Of course, the bank may not be able to immediately identify a counterparty with matching needs. In this case, the bank might want to construct temporary hedges using other instruments including such things as FRA and FXA contracts, futures contracts, and/or positions in Treasuries or foreign debt. We address these considerations more fully in Chapter 4.

In the event that the bank experiences a demand imbalance on one side of the currency swap market, the bank will find it necessary to raise or lower its midrate. For example, suppose that the bank experiences a surge in demand for currency swaps by clients who want to pay 5-year fixed-rate deutsche marks and receive floating-rate dollars. To discourage this side of the market and encourage the other, the bank will raise its 5-year midrate from 6.78 percent to say 6.85 percent.

Determining the correct midrates to serve as the basis of swap pricing is typically a function of a swap bank's international capital markets group. Capital market groups operate with an international perspective and continuously monitor the capital markets worldwide. They watch their own banks' swap portfolios closely and adjust rates quickly when they suspect that an imbalance is developing. A capital markets group may find, for instance, that they must lower the bank's 4-year midrate, while simultaneously raising the bank's 5-year midrate.

Currency Swaps With No Initial Exchange of Borrowing

The straight currency swap involves an initial exchange of principals and an eventual reexchange of principals. Not all currency swaps involve two exchanges of principals. Let's consider such a case.

Suppose it is now February 1, 1989. As a consequence of an earlier financing, a firm is committed to making semiannual floating-rate (six-month LIBOR) dollar payments on an amortizing loan for four more years. The payment dates are August 1 and February 1. By the nature of the firm's business, the firm receives revenue in deutsche marks. The firm's current payment schedule is depicted in Exhibit 3.10.

EXHIBIT 3.10

Date	Loan Balance Before Payment	LoanBalance After Payment	Payment Amount
1 Feb 1989		$4.0 million	———
1 Aug 1989	$4.0 million	$3.5 million	$0.5 million + LIBOR
1 Feb 1990	$3.5 million	$3.0 million	$0.5 million + LIBOR
1 Aug 1990	$3.0 million	$2.5 million	$0.5 million + LIBOR
1 Feb 1991	$2.5 million	$2.0 million	$0.5 million + LIBOR
1 Aug 1991	$2.0 million	$1.5 million	$0.5 million + LIBOR
1 Feb 1992	$1.5 million	$1.0 million	$0.5 million + LIBOR
1 Aug 1992	$1.0 million	$0.5 million	$0.5 million + LIBOR
1 Feb 1993	$0.5 million	$0.0	$0.5 million + LIBOR

Recent fluctuations in the DM/US exchange rate and U.S. interest rates have caused the firm's management to become increasingly concerned about its dollar liabilities and have led the firm to look for a way to convert its floating-rate dollar liabilities to fixed-rate deutsche mark liabilities. At the same time, it would like to lock in the current DM/US exchange rate (1.75 DM/US) for all future exchanges. The swap bank offers a currency swap with no initial exchange of principal. The bank offers to pay LIBOR on the amortizing balance and to pay the $0.5 million every six months. The swap has an average life of 2.5 years, and the bank's current midrate for 2.5-year deutsche marks is 6.365 percent. In exchange for the bank's paying LIBOR, the bank requires the firm to pay the bank 6.49 percent (midrate plus 12.5 bps). In addition, the bank will pay the firm $0.5 million every six months in exchange for the firm paying the bank 0.875 million deutsche marks every six months. This latter sum reflects principal translations at a DM/US exchange rate of 1.75. These payments are depicted in Exhibit 3.11.

EXHIBIT 3.11

Date	Bank Pays Counterparty Client	Counterparty Client Pays Bank
1 Feb 89	———	———
1 Aug 89	$0.5 million + LIBOR	DM 0.875 million + 6.49 percent
1 Feb 90	$0.5 million + LIBOR	DM 0.875 million + 6.49 percent
1 Aug 90	$0.5 million + LIBOR	DM 0.875 million + 6.49 percent
1 Feb 91	$0.5 million + LIBOR	DM 0.875 million + 6.49 percent
1 Aug 91	$0.5 million + LIBOR	DM 0.875 million + 6.49 percent
1 Feb 92	$0.5 million + LIBOR	DM 0.875 million + 6.49 percent
1 Aug 92	$0.5 million + LIBOR	DM 0.875 million + 6.49 percent
1 Feb 93	$0.5 million + LIBOR	DM 0.875 million + 6.49 percent

The counterparty client's dollar commitments to its earlier financing source (3rd-party lender) are now assured. The bank will pay its counterparty client $0.5 million + LIBOR flat every six months, and the counterparty client will then pay this identical sum to its creditor. The client's net liability is now to pay DM 0.875 million plus 6.49 percent sa. That is, it has a fixed-rate deutsche mark commitment—exactly what it was looking for. It is now fully hedged with respect to exchange rates and interest rates.

Unlike the straight currency swap, which is best understood as an exchange of borrowings, this currency swap is best viewed as a series of forward contracts all made at the current spot rate of 1.75 DM/US with the normal forward-spot exchange rate differential incorporated in the interest payments made by the counterparties.

Off-Market Pricing

Just as it is frequently necessary to make pricing adjustments to interest-rate swaps for such things as payment frequencies that differ from those assumed in the indication pricing schedules and for amortization schedules that differ from those assumed in the indication pricing schedules; it is also frequently necessary to make pricing adjustments for variations in currency swap requirements. The straight currency swap assumes semiannual payments and bullet transactions. If the currency swap required annual fixed-rate payments instead of semiannual payments, we would determine the annual equivalent rate for the semiannual rate by again using Equation 3.5. If the swap was amortizing, we would determine the appropriate rate to use by employing average life rather than maturity (as we did with the currency swap in the preceding example). There is one additional adjustment which is often necessary in the case of currency swaps. This occurs when the swap is **off-market**.

The need for an off-market swap arises when a firm has an existing liability at a rate that differs from the rate currently prevailing in the market. Consider the following case: A U.S. firm is committed to making semiannual interest payments to holders of its deutsche mark bonds which it issued five years ago. The bond principal covers DM 18 million all of which will be repaid at maturity in ten more years. The bond carries a fixed coupon of 9.50 percent. The U.S. firm would like to swap this liability for a floating-rate dollar liability. Its purpose is to eliminate exchange-rate risk. Note that this swap requires no initial exchange of principals and is similar in this regard to the case discussed in the preceding section.

The swap bank's current indication pricing schedule (Exhibit 3.6) calls for the bank to pay a fixed rate of DM 6.975 percent sa (midrate less 12.5 bps) against six-month LIBOR flat. However, the counterparty client, which is the U.S. firm in this case, requires the bank to pay DM 9.50 percent. Any rate other than DM 9.50 percent will leave a residual exchange-rate risk for the U.S. firm. This swap calls for off-market pricing.

The trick to pricing off-market swaps is to create cash flow patterns having equivalent present values. This requires that we exploit our knowledge of the 10-year U.S. fixed rate and the 10-year DM fixed rate. We use midrates for this purpose. The latter is 7.10 percent (Exhibit 3.6) and the former is 9.75 percent (Exhibit 3.1).

The first step is to determine the rate differential between what the bank's counterparty client requires and what the bank would ordinarily pay. The differential, in this case, is 2.525 percent (9.50 - 6.975). That is, the client requires that the bank pay a premium of 2.525 percent on the DM fixed-rate side.

The next step is to determine the dollar rate premium which has the same present value as this 2.525 percent DM premium. Since this DM payment takes the form of an annuity, we can compute the present value of the payment using present value annuity arithmetic. The necessary relationship is given by Equation 3.6.[10]

EQUATION 3.6

$$PVA = PMT \times [(1 - (1 + R/m)^{-m \cdot n}) \div R/m]$$

PVA: Present value of the annuity
PMT: Annuity payment
R: Midrate (for deutsche marks)
n: Term of swap (number of years to maturity of swap)
m: Frequency of interest payments

The values of PMT, R, m, and n are, in this case, 2.525, 7.10 percent, 2, and 10 respectively. Plugging these values into Equation 3.6 provides a present value of 35.725.

We now use this present value to determine the dollar interest premium. We again use Equation 3.6, but we now use the current midrate for dollars for R (9.75 percent) rather than the current midrate for deutsche marks. We substitute the value 35.725 for PVA and solve for PMT. The value of PMT that solves this particular case is 2.836. This value is interpreted as the dollar rate premium on this off-market transaction. However, this rate premium was derived from fixed-rate bond equivalent yields and, consequently, cannot be added directly to LIBOR. We use Equation 3.1 to make the necessary adjustment. The adjustment provides a yield premium of 2.797 percent that can be added directly to LIBOR. The swap will then call for the bank to pay its counterparty client deutsche marks at the semiannual fixed

rate of 9.50 percent in exchange for the counterparty client paying
the bank dollars at the rate of six-month LIBOR plus 2.797 percent.
At maturity, the parties will exchange principals at an exchange rate
of 1.75 DM/US (the spot rate at the time the swap is negotiated).
The cash flows associated with this swap are depicted in Exhibits
3.12 and 3.13. The bank may also look to collect a front-end fee if
any special financial engineering was required in designing the swap
or evaluating the client's needs.

EXHIBIT 3.12

OFF-MARKET PRICING OF CURRENCY SWAP
INTEREST FLOWS BETWEEN COUNTERPARTY AND
SWAP BANK

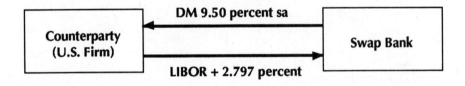

EXHIBIT 3.13

OFF-MARKET PRICING OF CURRENCY SWAP
TERMINAL POINT EXCHANGE OF PRINCIPALS

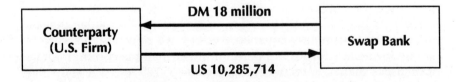

Note: In this swap, the only exchange of principals occurs at the termina-
        tion of the swap agreement. This exchange takes place at the spot rate
        which prevailed at the time the swap was negotiated, i.e., 1.75 DM/
        US.

The client firm is now fully hedged against exchange-rate fluctuations. The deutsche mark payments, including both interest and
principal, which it must make to its creditor (3rd-party lender) are
perfectly matched by the bank's payments to its client firm. The client
firm's net position consists of its LIBOR plus 2.797 percent payments
to the bank. It need no longer concern itself at all with the DM/US
exchange rate.

A Note on the Pricing of Circus Swaps

The swap pricing discussed in this chapter has provided for the
pricing of fixed-for-floating interest-rate swaps and fixed-for-floating currency swaps. The corporate user might require a swap to convert
fixed-rate payments in one currency to fixed-rate payments in another currency or, alternatively, to convert floating-rate payments in
one currency to floating-rate payments in another currency. As
mentioned in Chapter 2, fixed-for-fixed rate and floating-for-floating
rate currency swaps can be engineered by combining a fixed-for-floating rate interest-rate swap with a fixed-for-floating rate currency swap.
When both of the floating rates are LIBOR, these combinations are
often called **circus swaps.**

The pricing of circus swaps follows directly from the mechanics
of the two swap components. Consider one last time the off-market
swap discussed in the previous section. The U.S. firm has swapped a
9.50 percent fixed-rate deutsche mark commitment for LIBOR plus
2.797 percent. This same client can now convert its dollar floating-
rate payments to fixed-rate payments using the rates in Exhibit 3.1.
That is, the bank will pay its counterparty client LIBOR + 2.797 percent in exchange for the client paying the bank the "bank-receives"
rate of 9.92 percent plus 2.836 percent. The end result for the counterparty client is a fixed-rate semiannual payment of 12.756 percent US.

No additional adjustments for principal are required, since the
principal in an interest-rate swap is purely notional. The interest flows
from the currency portion of this off-market circus swap are depicted
in Exhibit 3.14 (this repeats Exhibit 3.12). The interest flows from the
interest-rate portion of the circus swap are depicted in Exhibit 3.15.
The net cash flows from the combined components of the circus swap
are depicted in Exhibit 3.16 (see next page).

EXHIBIT 3.14

OFF-MARKET CIRCUS SWAP
INTEREST FLOWS ON CURRENCY SWAP COMPONENT

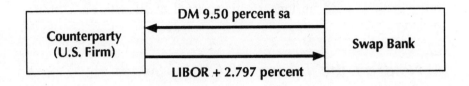

EXHIBIT 3.15

OFF-MARKET CIRCUS SWAP
INTEREST FLOWS ON INTEREST-RATE
SWAP COMPONENT

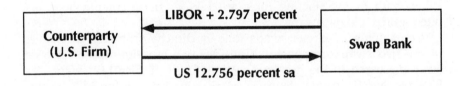

EXHIBIT 3.16

OFF-MARKET CIRCUS SWAP
NET INTEREST FLOWS FROM COMBINED COMPONENT

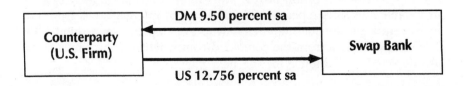

Summary

The pricing of swaps is a complex undertaking. Typically, a swap bank's capital markets group is charged with developing and periodically revising indicative swap pricing schedules for both the interest-rate and the currency swaps in which the bank makes a market. These schedules provide base rates. The base rates will be adjusted to reflect any special features the client requires, the creditworthiness of the client, the frequency of interest payments, and whether the swap will be at-market or off-market. The arithmetic of swap pricing depends heavily on the mathematics of the time value of money.

Indicative pricing schedules most often assume that swaps are nonamortizing. When this condition holds, the swap rates are determined as a spread over Treasury securities of similar maturity. When the swap involves amortization of principal, an alternative measure of the swap term must be used. The most frequently used of such measures is the average life of the swap.

The swap banker must monitor the bank's swap portfolio on a continuous basis. While temporary hedges are often constructed through positioning in the Government securities market, futures, and other hedging media, the optimal long-term goal is to match all swaps. This matching is often achieved by writing a swap with a second counterparty or by writing a swap with another swap bank on an interbank basis. When one side of the bank's swap portfolio becomes out of line with the other side, the bank can adjust its bid and asked prices to attract activity to the deficient side and/or make the surplus side less attractive.

A need for off-market pricing arises whenever a client of the bank requires a swap to be written at a rate which differs from the prevailing swap rates. This situation is most likely to arise when a firm seeks to transform the rate or currency type of an existing obligation. The off-market pricing adjustments are made via the vehicle of present value arithmetic.

Circus swaps, by combining interest-rate and currency swaps, allow the end user to convert fixed-rate debt in one currency to fixed-rate debt in a different currency or to convert floating-rate debt in one currency to floating-rate debt in another currency. These swaps are priced in exactly the same fashion as other swaps but the pricing is a two-stage process.

Terms

average life
bond equivalent yield
circus swaps
duration
front-end fee
grace period
indication pricing schedule
money market yield
off-market
on the runs
reinvestment risk
reverse repurchase agreement
semiannual rate
sinking fund
spread over Treasuries
transfer pricing rate (TPR)
yield curve
zero-coupon yield curve

REVIEW QUESTIONS

1. A firm would like to arrange an amortizing interest-rate swap having an initial notional principal of $12 million. There would be a two-year grace period during which no notional principal would be amortized. Beginning at the end of the third year, $2 million will be amortized each year for 6 years (years 3, 4, 5, 6, 7, and 8). Calculate the average life of this swap.

2. Suppose that a swap bank has the following indicative pricing schedule for fixed-for-floating interest rate swaps:

Maturity/ Average Life	——————Fixed Rate ——————		Current TN Yield
	Bank Pays	Bank Receives	
4.0 years	TN + 32 bps	TN + 48 bps	8.83 percent
4.5 years	TN + 36 bps	TN + 55 bps	8.88 percent
5.0 years	TN + 40 bps	TN + 58 bps	8.92 percent
5.5 years	TN + 40 bps	TN + 60 bps	8.94 percent
6.0 years	TN + 42 bps	TN + 60 bps	8.95 percent
7.0 years	TN + 44 bps	TN + 62 bps	8.96 percent

N.B.: All rates above are stated on a semiannual basis and assume bullet transactions. All quotes are against LIBOR flat.

Now, suppose that the firm in Problem 1 above wanted to be the fixed-rate payer (floating-rate receiver). What rate would the bank expect the firm to pay?

3. The rate which the firm in Problem 2 would pay is a semiannual rate. Suppose that the firm wanted to receive semiannual payments on the floating-rate side but wanted to make annual payments on the fixed-rate side. Determine the annual rate which is equivalent to the semiannual rate obtained in your answer to Problem 2.

4. Suppose that a firm has an existing nonamortizing French franc (FF) obligation with 7 years remaining on which it pays a semiannual rate of 11.2 percent. The firm would like to transform this fixed-rate FF obligation into a floating-rate dollar obligation. The firm approaches a swap bank which has the following indicative pricing schedule for French franc to dollar swaps:

Maturity/Average Life	Midrate (FF)
5 years	7.20 percent sa
7 years	7.35 percent sa
10 years	7.45 percent sa

N.B.: All quotes are against six-month LIBOR flat. The rates above are midrates. To the midrate add 10 bps when the bank is the fixed-rate receiver and deduct 10 bps when the bank is the fixed-rate payer.

To convert its fixed-rate FF obligation to a floating-rate dollar obligation, the firm needs an off-market swap. The firm wants the bank to pay it a semiannual FF rate of 11.2 percent for seven years. If the bank obliges, what premium (or discount) over LIBOR will the bank expect from the firm?

5. Suppose that the firm in Problem 4 above decides that it would like to convert its fixed-rate FF obligation into a fixed-rate dollar obligation. The bank has the fixed-for-floating FF to dollar currency swap schedule given in Problem 4 and the fixed-for-floating (dollar) interest-rate swap schedule given in Problem 2. If the bank agrees to pay the firm a semiannual FF rate of 11.2 percent, what fixed semiannual U.S. rate would the bank expect the firm to pay it?

6. A swap bank has just concluded a $20 million fixed-for-floating 6-year (average life) interest-rate swap. The bank has no immediate

prospect for matching this swap with another swap. Describe how the bank would hedge the swap using the Treasury cash market. Illustrate by means of cash flow diagrams.

7. Describe how a bank might encourage (or discourage) swap activity on one side of a fixed-for-floating interest-rate swap for any given average life. Apply this same logic to an imbalance in any given average life currency swap.

8. What considerations might lead a swap bank to impose a premium to its indicative pricing for swaps (that is, treat one client firm differently from others)?

9. Describe the concept of duration. What does it measure?

10. What role does the yield curve play in the pricing of swaps?

ENDNOTES

1. Interbank swaps are swaps made between banks in an effort to better manage their own swap portfolios.

2. The corporation will, of course, also encounter some flotation costs in the form of underwriting fees. While these flotation costs must be factored in to obtain the firm's all-in cost in any actual financing, we ignore them here in order to concentrate on the pricing of swaps.

3. For a fuller discussion of yield conversions and yield conventions, see Fage (1986).

4. When the swap bank's objective is simply to hedge a swap until a matched swap can be booked or until the swap can be assigned to another party, the bank will often hedge the swap in T-note and Eurodollar (or T-bill) futures. This is important as futures hedges, like swaps themselves, are off-balance sheet positions, while cash market positions are on-balance sheet positions. This use of futures to hedge unmatched swaps is discussed more fully in Chapter 4.

5. The liquidity premium theory explains the shape of the yield curve in terms of ever greater interest-rate risk associated with ever greater maturities on U.S. Treasury securities. Greater risk requires higher levels of interest as compensation.

6. See Macaulay [1938]. The Macaulay duration was later shown to be slightly biased and a second duration measure which corrects for this bias, called the modified duration, is now most often used for measuring interest-rate sensitivity. The modified duration is obtained by a simple adjustment to the Macaulay duration. The

   modified duration, denoted here as D_m is given by: $D_m = D/(1 + y)$, where D denotes the Macaulay duration and y denotes the instrument's present yield.
7. There is a long literature on the use of duration as a tool for measuring a debt instrument's price sensitivity to interest-rate fluctuations and an equally long literature on the use of duration in immunization and hedging strategies. Samples of this literature include: Maloney and Yawitz (1986), Arak, Goodman and Snailer (1986), Bierwag, Kaufman, and Toevs (1983), Gushee (1981), Khang (1979), Bierwag, Kaufman, and Khang (1978), and Grove (1974).
8. For an examination of the relationship between duration and average life, see Leibowitz (1986).
9. A sinking fund is a program involving the periodic set-aside of a fixed sum to provide for the eventual retirement of an outstanding debt or preferred stock issue.
10. For a discussion of the financial arithmetic of annuities, see Weston and Copeland (1986).

REFERENCES AND SUGGESTED READING

Arak, M., L. S. Goodman, and J. Snailer. "Duration Equivalent Bond Swaps: A New Tool." *Journal of Portfolio Management*, 26-32 (Summer 1986).

Bierwag, G. O., G. G. Kaufman, and C. Khang. "Duration and Bond Portfolio Analysis: An Overview." *Journal of Financial and Quantitative Analysis*, 671-679 (November 1978).

Bierwag, G. O., G. G. Kaufman, and A. Toevs. "Duration: Its Development and Use in Bond Portfolio Management." *Financial Analysts Journal* (July/August 1983).

Fage, P. *Yield Calculations, Credit Swiss First Boston Research* (October 1986).

Gay, G. D. and R. W. Kolb. "Removing Bias in Duration Based Hedging Models: A Note." *Journal of Futures Markets*, 4:2, 225-228 (Summer 1984).

Grove, M. A. "On Duration and the Optimal Maturity Structure of the Balance Sheet." *The Bell Journal of Economics* (Autumn 1974).

Gushee, C. H. "How to Hedge a Bond Investment." *Financial Analysts Journal*, 41-51 (March/April 1981).

Khang, C. "Bond Immunization when Short-term Rates Fluctuate More than Long-term Rates." *Journal of Financial and Quantitative Analysis* (December 1979).

Leibowitz, M. L. "The Dedicated Bond Portfolio in Pension Funds—Part II: Immunization, Horizon Matching and Contingent Procedures." *Financial Analysts Journal*, 47-57 (March/April 1986).

Macaulay, F. R. *Some Theoretical Problems Suggested by the Movement of Interests Rates, Bond Yields, and Stock Prices in the United States Since 1856* (New York: Columbia University Press for the National Bureau of Economic Research, 1938).

Maloney, K. J. and J. B. Yawitz. "Interest Rate Risk, Immunization, and Duration." *Journal of Portfolio Management*, 41-48 (Spring 1986).

Weston J. F. and T. E. Copeland. *Managerial Finance*, 8th ed. (New York: Dryden Press, 1986).

CHAPTER 4

MANAGING THE SWAP PORTFOLIO

Overview

In this chapter, we consider the management of a swap portfolio from the perspective of a market-maker swap bank. In our examination of the pricing of swaps in Chapter 3, we discussed the swap bank's sources of revenue from intermediating in swap finance. These included the bank's bid-asked spread and, to a lesser degree, front-end fees (for financial engineering and special features) that are charged to the counterparty client. While these revenue sources are of considerable importance in the management of a swap portfolio, further discussion of them would be largely redundant. Consequently, we concentrate our discussion in this chapter on the other key considerations in running a swap portfolio—identifying and quantifying the various risks to which the swap bank is exposed from its swap activity. This leads logically to a discussion of the hedging of swaps individually and the hedging of a swap portfolio.

The management of the risks associated with a swap portfolio is considerably more complex than is the management of the risks associated with a stock portfolio. While swap risks, like stock risks, contain both systematic and unsystematic components, the swap risks are not easily managed by simple diversification. Further, the non-diversifiable risks cannot be measured by simple criteria such as beta coefficients—which are often used to measure the systematic risk associated with common stock portfolios.[1] First, there are many different types of risks and these risks are related in complex ways. Second, the optimal hedge for a portfolio of booked swaps can and usually does change over time—even if no changes are made to the swap portfolio. Third, the legal rights of the counterparties to swaps vary from country to country. Finally, the tax and accounting treatment of swaps are not uniform from country to country—although considerable progress toward uniformity in bank accounting and capital requirements has been made recently. We will address all of these issues in this chapter.

Risk Exposure for the Swap Bank

We assume throughout this chapter that the swap bank is a swap dealer and not a speculator in swaps. That is, the bank looks to profit from its market-making activities alone. As a market maker, the bank does not take naked positions in swaps and looks to be fully hedged at all times. Thus, to the extent that the bank makes an effort to forecast interest rates and exchange rates, it does so (1) as a service to its clients, and (2) to more accurately quantify the risks associated with its swap portfolio.

The swap bank actually has two separate portfolio management problems. First, it must manage the risks associated with newly negotiated swaps until such time as those swaps can be matched against swaps with other counterparties. Second, the bank must manage the risks associated with its portfolio of matched swaps. Some risks are specific to the first portfolio problem and some to the second. Still other risks are important in the management of both portfolios. Swap risks are more interrelated than are the risks which characterize most other types of asset portfolios. We first discuss the different sources of risk and then discuss the relationships of these risks to each other. The risks we examine include: interest-rate risk, exchange-rate risk, credit risk, market risk, default risk, mismatch risk, basis risk, spread risk, sovereign risk, and delivery risk. We should point out that there is some inconsistency in the usage of these terms. For example, as we will point out again later, what we have called default risk in this text is sometimes called credit risk by some swap dealers.

Interest-Rate Risk

The inverse relationship between debt instrument yields and the prices of fixed-rate debt instruments is the source of interest-rate risk. All other things being equal, a change in the level of interest rates for debt of a given maturity will necessitate an equivalent change in the yield of all existing debt instruments of that same maturity.[2] This yield adjustment must take the form of a change in the instrument's price, since the coupon on a fixed-rate instrument is, by definition, fixed. This is, of course, also true for the swap coupon. Thus, a swap with a given term exposes the fixed-rate paying and receiving counter-parties to an interest-rate risk. The extent of the risk for the bank, the focus of this discussion, will depend on the degree to which the bank has offset the risk in other swaps or, alternatively, offset the risk in temporary hedges, while looking for matching swaps.

The floating-rate side of a swap will periodically adjust, called a reset, to the prevailing interest rate. The resets occur at discrete inter-vals, usually semiannually. The **reset dates** are specified in the terms of the swap agreement. Because the floating rate adjusts to prevail-ing market conditions, the floating-rate side of a swap is character-ized by significantly less interest-rate risk than is the fixed-rate side. This is not to imply that there is no interest-rate risk on the floating-rate side. As long as there is a lag between resets, there is some inter-est-rate risk. Nevertheless, the risk is small. For this reason, we concentrate our discussion on the management of the interest-rate risk associated with the fixed-rate side.

Consider a simple example in the context of an interest-rate swap: A swap bank enters a $100 million 10-year fixed-for-floating swap as receiver of the semiannual swap coupon. At the time, the bank's 10-year midrate is 10.50 percent. The bank will pay six-month LIBOR to Counterparty A. The bank's commitment is depicted in Exhibit 4.1. Immediately after negotiating the first swap, the bank begins the search for a second Counterparty (B) having matching needs with whom the bank will negotiate a mirror image commitment. A matched swap would have the cash flows depicted in Exhibit 4.2. The bank expects to earn 1/8 point on each side for a total of 25 bps on the combined swaps. This is depicted in Exhibit 4.3

Consider the bank's expected revenue from the matched swaps depicted in Exhibit 4.3 (we will ignore any front-end fees as these are increasingly rare). For purposes of the calculations, assume that Counterparty B is identified and signed without any lag and that the swaps are perfect matches. The bank earns 12.5 bps semiannually (25 bps annually) on $100 million. This is equivalent to $125,000. The present value of this cash-flow stream is calculated using present value annuity mathematics. Recall that only interest is exchanged. There is no exchange of notional principals on interest-rate swaps.

$$PVA = 125,000 \times [(1 - (1 + (0.105 \div 2))^{-2 \cdot 10}) \div (0.105 \div 2)]$$
$$= 1,525,278$$

EXHIBIT 4.1

**MATCHING SWAPS
INITIAL SWAP WITH COUNTERPARTY A**

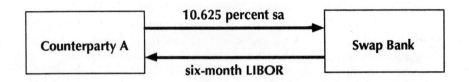

($100 million notional principal)

EXHIBIT 4.2

**MATCHING SWAPS
GOAL: A MATCHED SWAP WITH COUNTERPARTY B**

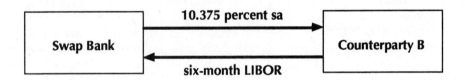

($100 million notional principal)

EXHIBIT 4.3

COMBINED CASH FLOWS FROM MATCHED SWAPS

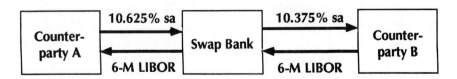

($100 million notional principal)   ($100 million notional principal)

Thus, the pair of swaps should earn the bank $1,525,278 in a present value sense before its administrative and other overhead costs. Suppose now that the bank does not hedge its interest-rate exposure while searching for the second counterparty; and, while the bank is looking, interest rates change—forcing the bank to revise its 10-year midrate. Consider what happens to the present value of the bank's revenues if the rate were to rise and also if the rate were to fall. These are depicted in Exhibits 4.4 and 4.5 (see pages 96–97), respectively. The present value of these outcomes is also depicted in the first line of Exhibit 4.6 on the assumption that the midrate rises by 50 basis points. The second line of Exhibit 4.6 indicates the present value had the initial swap called for the swap bank to pay fixed rate rather than receive fixed rate. These present values are calculated using the prevailing 10.5 percent midrate as the discount rate.

One can think of the bid-asked spread as a kind of cushion against interest-rate risk. For example, if the spread is 25 bps, as it is in the preceding example, the midrate could move 25 bps against the bank before the profit from the paired swaps is completely eliminated. It follows then that a narrower bid-asked spread means a smaller cushion. As the liquidity of the swap market has grown, there has been a substantial narrowing of the bid-asked spread and a concomitant decrease in the size of the interest-rate risk cushion.[3]

EXHIBIT 4.6

| On Initial Swap | ------ Present Value of Cash Flows if ------ | | |
	No Change	*MidRate* *Rises 50 bps*	*Falls 50 bps*
Bank Receives Fixed Rate	$1,525,278	-$1,525,278	$4,575,834
Bank Pays Fixed Rate	$1,525,278	$4,575,834	-$1,525,278

Exchange-Rate Risk

Just as there is an interest-rate risk whenever there is an unhedged fixed-rate commitment, there is also an exchange-rate risk whenever there is an exchange-rate commitment. Consider an example: A U.S.-based swap bank agrees to a nonamortizing 5-year exchange of borrowings with a French firm. The swap bank would provide the French firm with US 25 million, and the firm would provide the bank with FF 100 million. The spot exchange rate at the time the swap is written is 4.000 FF/US. This can be stated equivalently as 0.2500 US/FF.

EXHIBIT 4.4

PRESENT VALUE OF PAIRED SWAPS IF RATES RISE
(BANK IS FIXED-RATE RECEIVER ON INITIAL SWAP)

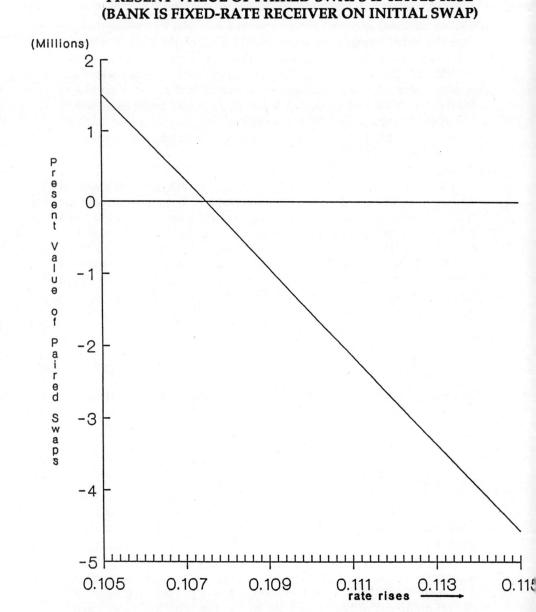

Midrate When Matched Swap is Identified

EXHIBIT 4.5

PRESENT VALUE OF PAIRED SWAPS IF RATES FALL
(BANK IS FIXED-RATE RECEIVER ON INITIAL SWAP)

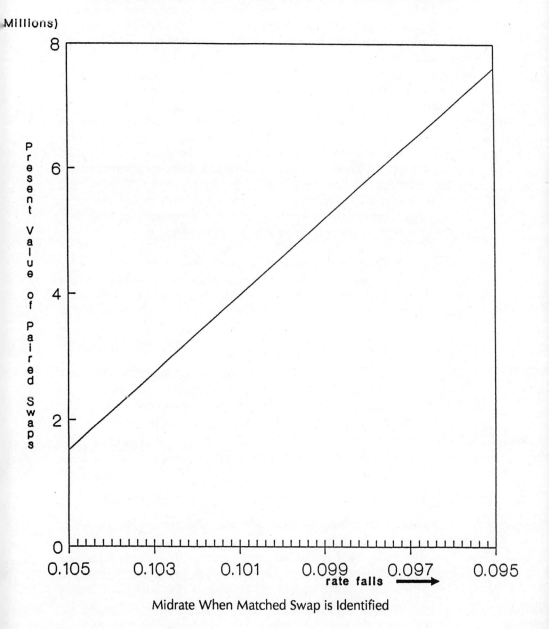

Midrate When Matched Swap is Identified

We employ the latter in this example. The bank's five-year midrate is FF 11.375 percent. The French firm agrees to pay six-month LIBOR, and the bank agrees to pay the French firm a semiannual rate of FF 11.25 percent. The swap coupon is found by deducting 1/8 point from the midrate. Suppose now that the bank carries the swap unhedged while it looks for a matched swap.

The swap bank runs the risk that the exchange rate of dollars for francs will change unfavorably while it is looking for a counterparty with matching needs. Suppose now that, within a few days, the bank is able to locate a counterparty with matched needs. In the interim, the spot exchange rate has declined to 0.2375 US/FF. Thus, on the matched swap, the bank's counterparty provides the bank with US 23.75 million, and the bank provides this second counterparty with FF 100 million. The bank must now secure the additional US 1.25 million elsewhere. There is a cost to the bank associated with obtaining the required funds. Most likely, the bank's swap division will obtain funds from other divisions of the bank at a price. The price for funds for intrabank transfers is called the **transfer pricing rate (TPR)**. This rate is sometimes called the **cost of carry**.

In this particular case, there is both an exchange-rate risk and an interest-rate risk. To make matters worse, these risks are positively correlated. All other things being equal, higher interest rates generally mean stronger currencies, and lower interest rates generally mean weaker currencies. Since the franc fell vis-a-vis the dollar, it is highly likely that French interest rates also fell relative to the dollar. Suppose that, at the time the second swap is written, the bank's 5-year semiannual midrate is FF 10.375 percent. The second counterparty agrees to pay the bank FF 10.50 percent in exchange for the bank paying the second counterparty six-month LIBOR. Thus, the net result is that the bank is receiving FF 10.50 percent and paying FF 11.25 percent. The bank has lost on both the exchange-rate and the interest-rate fronts.

Credit Risk

Different swap banks define credit risk differently. For example, for purposes of the discussion which follows, we define credit risk as the probability that a counterparty client will default. We then multiply this probability by market risk (which is defined in the next section) to obtain a dollar value called default risk (discussed later).

Many swap banks use the term credit risk to mean what we have called default risk. These usage differences of the terms "credit risk" and "default risk" are less important than the concepts involved and the methods of measurement employed. Nevertheless, the student of swaps should be aware of these differences in usage.

Credit risk is the risk that the bank's counterparty to a swap will be unable to fulfill its obligations due to bankruptcy, supervening illegality, change in the tax or accounting laws relative to those applicable at the time the swap was originated, and so on. As an intermediary between two matched swaps, the swap bank is independently obligated to both counterparties. That is, while the termination provisions of its swap with Counterparty A will release the bank from its obligation to make payments to Counterparty A should Counterparty A default on its obligation to the bank, the termination provisions with A do not release the bank from its obligations to Counterparty B.

Credit risk is generally regarded as the single most significant risk for swap banks. Fortunately, it is a risk which can be significantly reduced by diversification and other portfolio management strategies which we examine shortly.

Credit risk is closely related to two other forms of risk: market risk and mismatch risk. We consider these below. For the moment, we assume that the default on the part of one of the bank's counterparties will force the bank to seek a **replacement swap**. Ideally, a replacement swap would have terms identical to those of the defaulted swap. Unfortunately, it is highly probable that market conditions will have changed since the time the defaulted swap was originated. As such, the bank must seek a replacement swap which involves off-market pricing. The bank may have to pay (or receive) a front-end fee for such a swap. Calculating the size of the monetary inducement necessary to obtain a replacement swap on the same terms as the defaulted swap is called **marking-to-market**. Banks have routinely marked their swaps to market in an effort to assess their default exposure. Marking-to-market is now required as part of recently enacted bank capital adequacy rules. We will address these rules later.

Market Risk

Market risk refers to the difficulty of finding a counterparty with matched needs. Generally, the longer the maturity the thinner the market and the greater the market risk. When a market is thin, the bank can demand a greater spread from a counterparty client who approaches the bank. On the other hand, when the bank does a swap with one counterparty in a thin market, it may have to make concessions to attract another swap counterparty for an offsetting swap. As with credit risk, there are usage differences in terminology with market risk. Some swap dealers regard these risks as manifestations of mismatch risks. We define mismatch risk more specifically later.

Because markets tend to be thinnest in the longer maturity swaps, the swaps with the greatest market risk also tend to exhibit the greatest interest-rate risk. Thus market risk and interest-rate risk are closely related. Indeed, many swap practitioners do not make a distinction between these forms of risk.

Market risk is related to credit risk. Should a counterparty default on its obligations to the bank, the bank must seek a replacement swap. The financial injury to the bank from such a default will depend on market conditions at the time. For example, suppose that three years into a seven year $40 million nonamortizing fixed-for-floating interest-rate swap, Counterparty A, which is paying a semiannual swap coupon of 10.35 percent against the bank's six-month LIBOR, defaults. The bank had matched this swap with a swap to another counterparty on which the bank is paying a swap coupon of 10.15 percent. Consequently, the bank is forced to find a replacement swap with terms similar to those of the defaulted swap. Since the original swap was written, interest rates have declined. Current market conditions dictate a midrate for a four-year fixed-for-floating rate swap of 8.75 percent. With the bank's 1/8 point premium, the counterparty would pay the bank a semiannual coupon of 8.875 percent against the bank's paying six-month LIBOR.

The bank should be able to induce a counterparty to accept the swap on the same terms as the defaulted swap if the bank pays the replacement counterparty a sum equal to the present value of the difference between the initial swap coupon and the prevailing swap rate. This is a semiannual rate differential of 1.475 percent (10.35 - 8.875) on $40 million of notional principal. This sum would be discounted at the current midrate of 8.75 percent sa. The present value of this sum is $1,955,762. This is the extent of the financial injury caused by the default of Counterparty A. This is a simple application of the off-market pricing discussed in Chapter 3. The sums which have to be paid (received) to induce a fixed-rate paying counterparty to enter a swap at a coupon above (below) the prevailing market rate is sometimes called a **buy-up** (**buy-down**).

Default Risk

Default risk measures the bank's combined exposure from credit risk and market risk. For example, suppose that, at the time a given swap is contemplated, the swap bank estimates that there is a 4 percent probability that a specific prospective counterparty will default on a $20 million 3-year nonamortizing fixed-for-floating interest-rate swap. The bank also estimates the economic harm to the bank, based on various projected future market conditions, should the counterparty default after 1 year, 2 years, and 3 years. The combination of credit risk (probability of default) and market risk (financial injury in the event of default) determines the bank's default risk.

Mismatch Risk

Swap banks make markets in swaps by accommodating their clients' needs. If a swap bank insisted on matching every provision of every pair of swaps to which it serves as an intermediary, it would have a very difficult time finding counterparties. Furthermore, even if it can induce a prospective counterparty to take a swap on the bank's terms, the bank will likely find that it must agree to pricing concessions in the form of a front-end fee paid to the second counterparty client.

For these reasons, swap banks generally do not insist on exact pairing of swap provisions. Instead, the swap bank running a swap portfolio will focus on the overall character of the portfolio rather than the character of the individual swaps.

Mismatches, which can include mismatches with respect to notional principal, maturity, the swap coupon, the floating index, the reset dates for the floating index, the payment frequencies, and the payment dates, expose the bank to some additional risk—especially if a counterparty defaults. This risk is called **mismatch risk**. Consider the following possibility: Suppose that a bank agrees to pay a counterparty six-month LIBOR on a notional principal of $30 million. Payment dates are January 30 and July 30. The counterparty will pay the bank a single annual payment at a rate of 9.80 percent. This payment is to be made each year on July 30. When payment dates on an interest-rate swap are matched, the counterparties only need pay (or receive) the interest differential. But, when the payment dates are mismatched, as they are in this example, the full interest payment must be made, at least on the unmatched dates. Suppose now that the bank pays $1.2 million in interest to the counterparty on January 30. The counterparty is not due to make any payments to the bank before July 30. Now suppose that the counterparty defaults on its obligation to the bank at the time it is to make its first payment on July 30. The counterparty's default releases the bank from its obligation to make its second payment to the counterparty; but, the bank must now resort to legal channels to recover its earlier payment to the counterparty. The bank will likely find itself in the position of a general creditor in the proceedings that follow.

As a second example of mismatch risk, consider mismatched reset dates. Suppose the initial swap is made when LIBOR is 6.5 percent. Several days elapse before a matched swap can be arranged. In the interim, LIBOR has risen to 7.20 percent. The bank is now locked into a significant payment mismatch until at least the next reset date.

Basis Risk

The **basis** is the difference between two prices. In the case of interest-rate swaps, the basis is the difference between two different floating-rate indexes. **Basis risk** is the risk that the two indexes might fluctuate relative to each other. Basis risk can arise in two ways. In the first, the counterparty requires a floating-for-floating rate swap, but the two sides of the swap are pegged to different indexes. This is depicted in Exhibit 4.7 for a floating-for-floating interest-rate swap involving three-month LIBOR and six-month LIBOR. In the second, two separate counterparties do a fixed-for-floating rate swap with the bank, but the floating rates are pegged to different indexes. This is depicted in Exhibit 4.8 for fixed-for-floating interest-rate swaps involving the six-month T-bill rate and six-month LIBOR.

This particular combination is quite common—both in the context of swaps and in other forms of financial spreading. Indeed, many of these spreads are so common, they have been given special names. For example, the spread between the T-bill rate and LIBOR for the same maturities is called, in market parlance, the **TED spread**. The term is drived from T-bills and Eurodollars, since LIBOR is the interest rate paid on Eurodollar deposits.

Suppose that, initially, LIBOR is 9.5 percent, and the T-bill rate is 8.5 percent. If the 1 percent (100 bps) rate differential were absolutely fixed, there would be no basis risk to the bank. But, the differential is not absolutely fixed. It might be that the rate differential between LIBOR and the T-bill rate has been as small as 10 bps and as large as 140 bps in recent years. These fluctuations are the source

EXHIBIT 4.7

BASIS RISK: FLOATING-FOR-FLOATING
INTEREST-RATE SWAP

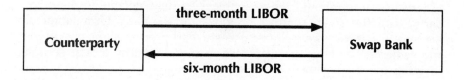

EXHIBIT 4.8

BASIS RISK: TWO FIXED-FOR-FLOATING
INTEREST-RATE SWAPS

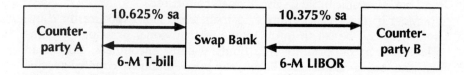

of basis risk. In this particular case, basis risk is measured as the variance of the TED spread.

In the language of statistics, basis risk exists when the two indexes are less than **perfectly correlated**. It is for this reason that the effectiveness of a hedge is routinely measured in terms of the degree of correlation between the two indexes.

Sovereign Risk

Sovereign risk arises in currency swaps. It is a reflection of a country's financial standing in the world community. To some degree, it is a function of the country's political stability and historic performance in meeting its international financial obligations. The greater the probability that a government may impose foreign-exchange controls, thus making it impossible for a counterparty to honor its commitments, the greater is the **sovereign risk**. This is one form of a condition called **supervening illegality**.

In the event that an illegality should arise, the counterparties to a swap have the right to terminate the swap subject to an attempt by the affected party to assign the swap to a branch or an affiliate located in a jurisdiction in which there is no illegality. Should the nature of the illegality, or the terms of the contract prevent such a change of jurisdiction, or should the assignment be unacceptable to the other party, then the swap contract provides for the early termination of the swap on a two-way payment basis. Early termination provisions and settlement options are discussed in more detail in a later section covering the management of credit risk.

Because the existence of sovereign risk affects a counterparty's creditworthiness, many analysts simply regard it as another aspect of credit risk. This is a mistake. Credit risk is counterparty specific, while sovereign risk is country specific. Thus, all swaps made with counterparties in the same country share sovereign risk. Routine diversification, which can substantially reduce credit risk, will do little to reduce sovereign risk unless an extra step is taken to ensure that the diversification is also across countries.

Most banks set strict limits to their allowable exposure by country. These can be set in terms of the total notional principal or some other criteria. Importantly, the limits usually encompass more than just the swap exposure. They may also embody country-specific exposures to the bank from its positions in FRAs, FXAs, general credit, and so on. This is important as the bank's exposures to sovereign risk (and foreign exchange risk) are correlated across all its positions in any one country or any one currency.[4]

Spread Risk

Spread risk is the risk that during the time between the origination of one swap and the subsequent origination of a matched swap the bank's spread over the relevant Treasury maturity may change. This should not be confused with interest-rate risk. To make the difference clear, let's suppose that at the time the bank originates the first swap, the bank prices the "bank-pays-fixed-rate-side" of a 5-year swap at the 5-year T-note rate plus 70 basis points. By the time the bank originates the matched swap, it has changed its pricing on the bank-pays-fixed-rate-side to the 5-year T-note rate plus 74 basis points. Even if there were no change in the T-note rate, there has been a change in the bank's cost. It is this possibility which constitutes spread risk. On the other hand, a change in the T-note rate would be a manifestation of interest-rate risk.

Delivery Risk

The final risk we discuss is **delivery risk**, also called settlement risk. This risk exists when payments are made between counterparties who must effect their payments to each other at different times of the day due to different settlement hours between the capital markets of the two parties. This most often occurs when the payments are made between counterparties in two different countries. For example, the Japanese capital markets close for the day before the U.S. markets open.

Delivery risk is greatest in currency swaps at the time of the exchanges of principals. Though this risk can be considerable, it can be managed. For example, many banks place a limit on the size of the allowable daily settlement with any one party. In some cases, banks make their exchanges through a neutral third party which does not make payment to either involved party until payments have been received from both parties. When the currencies are the same, delivery risk is considerably less than it first appears because the swap agreement usually requires the counterparties to make net payments rather than gross payments. That is, only the difference in the value of the payments needs to be exchanged with the higher value-paying party making a payment to the lower value-paying party equal to the difference in the values to be exchanged. Thus, **netting** payments significantly reduces the delivery exposure of both parties to a swap. Because it is so easily managed, we do not discuss this risk any further.

Quantifying the Exposure

It is not enough to simply identify the risks to which the bank is exposed when it books a swap. It is also important to quantify the exposure associated with swaps for at least four reasons. First, the greater the collective risks associated with booking a swap, the greater the compensation the swap bank should require from its counterparty client. This compensation may take the form of a front-end fee but will usually take the form of a larger coupon if the bank is receiving fixed rate or a smaller coupon if the bank is paying fixed rate. Second, the bank will need to hedge the hedgeable risks (including interest-rate risk, exchange-rate risk, and possibly basis risk) until such times as matched swaps can be negotiated. Formulation of the optimal hedge requires a quantification of the risks which are the subject of the hedge. Third, as suggested by portfolio theory, many risks will be, at least to some degree, offsetting so that the total risk associated with the bank's portfolio will be substantially less than the sum of the risks individually. This tendency for certain risks to be coincidentally offsetting is sometimes called a **natural hedge**. Accurate assessment of these risks requires quantification. Finally, the bank's internal policy, as well as regulatory compliance, will likely require some objective assessment of the risks and some explicit limitations to the risks that can be taken with respect to a single counterparty or a group of related counterparties.

As a general rule, management teams set the maximum allowable risk that the firm can bear. These risk levels have several dimensions. Risk limits are set by individual counterparties, maturities, types of exposure, and as noted earlier, by country—to mention a few. Most swap banks assign the measurement of risk exposures to risk management specialists. These important operatives monitor both the absolute size of the individual exposures and the portfolio implications of the risks. They then make pricing recommendations, devise and execute hedging strategies, and formulate policies to encourage or discourage specific swaps in order to bring about a better portfolio balance.

We have considered the quantification of interest-rate risk in the context of a simple example when we discussed this form of risk in an earlier section. We can quantify exchange-rate risk in a similar fashion. We take these issues up again when we discuss the hedging of these risks. For now, we concentrate on quantifying default risk (encompassing both credit and market risks) and mismatch risk.

Quantifying Default Risk

As mentioned earlier, default risk encompasses both credit risk and market risk. Credit risk is an objective assessment of the likelihood that a prospective counterparty will default. Market risk is a quantitative estimate of the financial injury which will be experienced should the client default. We consider the quantification of these latter risks individually, and then we combine them to obtain the default-risk exposure.

A bank with a long history in the credit markets has considerable experience estimating the likelihood that potential clients will default on their financial obligations. All such banks have extensive training programs for credit managers. The assessment of credit risks includes an examination of the potential counterparty's financial statements, financial history, its management's track record, collateralization of the obligation, and other pertinent factors. Some banks rely heavily on point scoring systems. Others use regression and **discriminant analysis.**[5] Some banks take a much more subjective approach, relying heavily on their own managers' personal knowledge of the client firm and its management.

All banks with substantial involvement in the swap markets devote considerable resources to economic forecasting. This will always include the forecasting of interest rates and exchange rates and will usually involve the forecasting of economic trends generally and industry trends more narrowly.

Let's assume, for purposes of an example, that a client has approached our swap bank for a $30 million 3-year nonamortizing fixed-for-floating interest-rate swap. The client firm would pay an annual fixed-rate coupon, and the bank would pay 1-year LIBOR. Using its credit expertise, management determines that the probability of the client defaulting within a year is negligible, but that there is a 1.25 percent probability that this client will default after 1 year (but before 2 years), and a 2 percent probability that the client will default after 2 years (but before 3 years). The bank's current midrate for an interest-rate swap of this maturity is 9.73 percent. To this, the bank adds or subtracts 1/8 point depending on whether the client is paying or receiving fixed rate.

Next, the bank attempts to determine the market risk should the client default. This requires some assumptions as to the course of future interest rates. Some banks simply assume some number of basis points above and below the current midrate for each year forward that rates must be projected (Method 1 below). Other banks make more complex estimates of the rates that might prevail and the probabilities associated with each of the possible rates (Method 2 below). These two methods are contrasted in Exhibit 4.9.

For purposes of this example, we assume the simpler of the two methods—Method 1. The market risk is measured as the present value of the rate differential encountered in negotiating a replacement swap should the counterparty client default. We use the current midrate to discount the rate differential. The present value is determined using the present value annuity formula (remembering that the payments are made annually in this specific case).

$$PVA = \$30 \text{ million} \times \text{rate change} \times [(1 - (1.0973)^{-Y}) \div .0973]$$

where: Y denotes the years *remaining* on this swap at the time of default.

The resultant values are summarized in Exhibit 4.10. These values represent the change in revenue relative to the expected revenue from the swap under each interest-rate state.

EXHIBIT 4.9

COMPARISON OF INTEREST-RATE FORECASTING TECHNIQUES

	Method I		Method II		
	Decrease	Increase	Rate Change	Probability (%)	
				Yr 1	Yr 2
Year 1	70 bps	70 bps	-250 bps	0.5	2.5
			-200 bps	2.5	4.5
Year 2	110 bps	110 bps	-150 bps	5.0	8.0
			-100 bps	9.5	12.0
			- 50 bps	20.0	15.0
			0 bps	25.0	16.0
			50 bps	20.0	15.0
			100 bps	9.5	12.0
			150 bps	5.0	8.0
			200 bps	2.5	4.5
			250 bps	0.5	2.5

EXHIBIT 4.10

MARKET EXPOSURE IN THE EVENT OF DEFAULT

		Profit (+) or Loss (-) (market risk) from Interest Rate Change	
If default occurs after:		Rates decrease	Rates increase
1 Year	(Y=2)	-$365,788 (-70 bps)	+$365,788 (+70 bps)
2 Years	(Y=1)	-$300,738 (-110 bps)	+$300,738 (+110 bps)

We interpret Exhibit 4.10 as follows: If rates fall and the client defaults after making its first swap payment, the bank will suffer a loss of $365,788. This is the amount the bank would have to pay a replacement counterparty to enter a swap on the same terms as the defaulted swap. If rates rise and the client defaults after making its first swap payment, the bank enjoys a windfall gain of $365,788. This is the amount the bank could ask of a replacement counterparty to accept a swap on the same terms as the defaulted swap. The values for the second year are interpreted similarly.

Remember that the losses and gains above only occur if the counterparty defaults. As mentioned earlier, the swap bank has estimated the likelihood of such an occurrence. The estimate is that the probability of a default after 1 year is 1.25 percent and the probability of a default after 2 years is 2 percent.[6] The default exposure is then found by multiplying the market exposure by the probability of default. This appears in Exhibit 4.11.

EXHIBIT 4.11

DEFAULT-RISK EXPOSURE

If default occurs after:	Default-risk exposure from an interest-rate change	
	Rates Decrease	Rates Increase
1 Year	-$4,572	+$4,572
2 Years	-$6,015	+$6,015

Notice that the default exposure is considerably less than the market exposure for the simple reason that the bank does not expect its counterparty to default. On the basis of the default exposure, the bank can be expected to adjust its pricing by adding a risk premium. In most financial situations, risk is measured in terms of **volatility** of an outcome around an expected outcome. Volatility, in turn, is usually measured as the standard deviation of the outcome. Using this logic, the size of the risk premium would be determined on the basis of the volatility of the default exposure. Some banks prefer to consider only **downside risk**, i.e., the financial harm resulting from a default if interest rates have moved in an unfavorable direction. They argue that a counterparty client is unlikely to default on a swap on which it has a positive mark-to-market value even if it is bankrupt. To do so would be to knowingly discard value. On the other hand, swap contracts typically include a specification of **termination events** and **events of default**. The occurrence of such an event will generally bring the contract's default provisions into play. One such event would be bankruptcy. For these reasons, we will assume equal likelihood of a default on a swap having positive mark-to-market value as on one having a negative mark-to-market value.[7]

All other things being equal, the larger the swap bank's default exposure, the greater the spread the bank will quote. For purposes of the example, we assume the bank measures its exposure in terms of volatility. Assuming equal likelihood of an increase and a decrease in interest rates, the standard deviation of the exposures are depicted in Exhibit 4.12.

EXHIBIT 4.12

VOLATILITY OF EXPOSURE (STANDARD DEVIATION)

If default occurs after	Standard Deviation
1 Year	4,572
2 Years	6,015

Variance = ΣProb[Exposure] x (Exposure - Mean)^2

Standard Deviation = Variance$^{1/2}$

It is important to appreciate the portfolio implications of default risks. Default risks are not highly correlated. This is not to suggest that they are completely uncorrelated. Most firms will be affected, to some degree, by economic conditions generally. But the correlations are likely to be quite low. Further, because the bank is a fixed-rate payer on half the swaps and a fixed-rate receiver on half the swaps, collectively, the default risks may be viewed as uncorrelated.[8]

For purposes of continuing the example, assume that the swap bank writes N identical matched swaps ($1/2 \cdot N$ pairs of swaps). The bank has the same default exposure (standard deviation, σ) to each counterparty. From a portfolio perspective, the per-swap default risk (standard error of the mean, σ_μ) declines as the number of swaps in the swap portfolio increases. The relationship is given by Equation 4.1.

EQUATION 4.1

$$\sigma_\mu = \frac{\sigma}{\sqrt{N}}$$

The per swap default exposure can now be seen to decline as the size of the portfolio grows. This is depicted in Exhibit 4.13. The behavior of the default risk makes it clear that default risk is largely an unsystematic risk.

EXHIBIT 4.13

BEHAVIOR OF PER-SWAP DEFAULT RISK

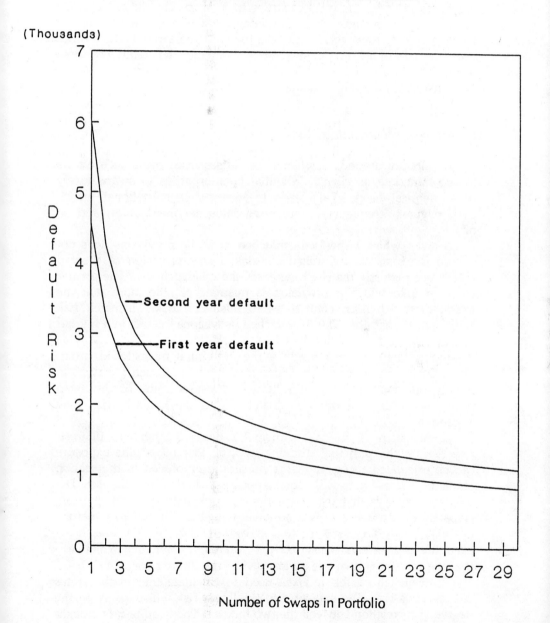

(Thousands)

Default Risk

Second year default

First year default

Number of Swaps in Portfolio

It is important to realize that, while default risk on a swap is small for a swap dealer, there is still considerable default risk exposure to the third-party lenders (investors) who provide the underlying funds used by the counterparties to a swap. The default risk for these parties is separate from the default risk to the swap dealer. At the same time, however, to the degree that the swap hedges other financial risks of a firm, the swap should enhance the creditworthiness of the firm in the eyes of its lenders (investors). This credit enhancement may afford some benefits for the firm.

Quantifying Mismatch Risk

As already argued, mismatch risk arises from the bank's efforts to accommodate its clients. Potential counterparties to swaps rarely have identical needs. This leads to mismatches in notional principals, payment frequencies, rate reset dates, payment dates, and so on.

A swap which is perfectly matched in all its provisions does not expose the bank to any mismatch risk. Every provision of a swap that is not perfectly matched increases the mismatch risk. The greater the degree to which a provision is mismatched, the more that the mismatched provision contributes to mismatch risk. Mismatch risk is difficult to quantify. The mismatched provisions interact in a myriad of ways. Some mismatched provisions may interact in such a way as to amplify the risks produced by the individual mismatched provisions. Other mismatched provisions may interact in such a way as to mollify one another. It would help to consider some of the swap provisions which are often mismatched and the kinds of risk they engender.

A mismatch of notional principal exposes the bank to interest-rate risk on the principal discrepancy. The amount of this exposure can be calculated using the same procedure employed in the section entitled "Interest Rate Risk" that appears earlier in this chapter. The only difference is that the calculation is applied to the principal discrepancy rather than the full notional principal. Mismatched maturities also create an exposure to interest-rate risk. In this case, however, the exposure is measured only on those payments which follow the termination of the swap having the shorter maturity.

A mismatch of the indexes used to calculate the floating rates creates basis risk. The exposure to this basis risk will depend on the degree of correlation between the two indexes. The floating-rate indexes can differ in either of two ways: The floating rates can be tied to different instruments, e.g., six-month LIBOR and six-month C.D. rate; or the floating rates can be tied to the same index but with different maturities, e.g., six-month LIBOR and three month LIBOR. Careful study of historic spread relationships, spread volatility and a forecast of the future spread can be used to quantify this risk.

Payment frequency mismatches create an exposure in the event of default. The quantification of this exposure has been addressed previously.

For plain vanilla swaps, the final consideration is the floating rate reset dates. The reset date is the date the floating rate is set for the next payment period. A difference of only one day will introduce some interest-rate risk. The greater the number of days by which the reset dates differ, the greater the interest-rate risk. Fortunately, this form of risk is easily diversified away. As a swap portfolio gets larger, it becomes increasingly less **date sensitive.**

Specialty swaps, including callable swaps, putable swaps, extendable swaps, amortizing swaps with grace periods, forward swaps, delayed rate-setting swaps, rate-cap swaps, and so on, introduce a great many mismatch complications. To some degree these problems can be solved by matching a provision in one swap with a provision in a different swap that is not part of the first pair of swaps. Alternatively, the swap bank can buy the necessary offsetting provisions from the counterparty to the matched swap. The cost of this purchase should be passed on to the party desiring the specialty feature. For example, suppose Counterparty A wants the right to extend a four-year swap for another three years at Counterparty A's option. Counterparty B has a matched need, but Counterparty B has no desire to have its swap extended. The bank can offer to purchase the right to extend the swap with Counterparty B for an additional three years. Suppose that Counterparty B agrees to provide such an option for a front-end payment of $0.5 million. The bank would then provide Counterparty A with the right to extend its swap with the bank for an additional front-end fee of at least $0.5 million. The value that Counterparty B and other potential counterparties place on the specialty provision affords some insight into the value of that provision. In an efficient market, this value should be representative of the exposure.

Managing Swap Risks

We have argued that certain risks associated with managing a swap portfolio are considerable when the swaps are viewed individually. Yet, when viewed collectively these same risks can be negligible.

This is typical of default risk. In the language of traditional portfolio theory, we say such risks are unsystematic. Diversification of the swap portfolio dramatically reduces unsystematic risks as the size of the portfolio becomes large. Other unsystematic risks include the reset-date risk component of mismatch risk, and the basis risk when floating rates are tied to different indexes.

Hedging Interest-Rate Risks

The preceding discussion serves to emphasize the importance of the character of the portfolio as a whole in assessing and measuring risk exposures. Ideally, each and every swap should be matched individually. But, from a pragmatic perspective, this is not possible. Risks that are not offset by matched swaps should be hedged whenever possible. It is not necessary, and it is not cost effective, to hedge unmatched swaps individually. It is more efficient to consider the degree to which the unmatched individual swap exposures are offsetting and then to hedge only the residual risk. It should be noted that hedging an individual swap or a portfolio of swaps exposes the swap bank to another kind of risk. In the language of hedging theory, this risk is called basis risk. The term basis risk, as used in hedging theory, is more broadly interpreted than the more narrow usage we employed in our use of this same term to describe the risk associated with tying two floating rate swaps to different indexes.[9]

A bank can hedge residual interest-rate risk in Treasury securities, as discussed in Chapter 3, or in interest-rate futures. Hedging in Treasury securities is attractive when the Treasury positions will serve as an intermediate-term to long-term substitute for a matched swap. When the objective is a very short-term hedge, interest-rate futures, including Treasury bond, note, and bill futures and Eurodollar futures, may be a better, more cost-effective hedge. We will consider an example of hedging of interest-rate risk by a swap bank having the latter objective. The bank negotiates new swap deals throughout the day. For simplicity, we only consider plain vanilla interest-rate swaps. The swaps are priced as a spread over Treasuries. The risk management department uses a **duration-based hedging model**.[10] The hedge ratio is found by first dividing the swap's duration D_s (using the swap's coupon as the yield) by the duration of the hedging instrument D_h. This duration ratio is then multiplied by the ratio of the current price of the swap as a percentage of its notional principal P_s (this is \$1 for all new swaps written "at market") and the current market price of $1 face value of the hedging instrument P_h. That is, the hedge ratio is given by:

$$HR = \frac{D_s}{D_h} \times \frac{P_s}{P_h}$$

The size of the hedge is then calculated by multiplying the swap's notional principal by the hedge ratio. This is translated into a given number of futures by dividing by the face value of the futures instrument. In the case of T-notes and T-bond futures, this face value is $0.1 million. In the case of Eurodollar and T-bill futures, this face value is $1 million. Suppose that T-note futures are currently priced at 95 percent of par. While the bank hedges both the fixed-rate side (in T-note and/or T-bond futures) and the floating-rate side (in Eurodollar and/or T-bill futures), we illustrate the hedging program for the fixed-rate side of a swap only.

Suppose, also for simplicity, that the bank starts the current day with no unmatched swaps. The first swap is finalized at 9:15 AM. The risk-management department is immediately notified that the swap has a maturity of 5 years and a notional principal of $30 million. The bank is the fixed-rate receiver. The risk-management department determines that the swap has a duration of 3.15 years. The T-note futures, which the bank uses to hedge all swaps with average lives of 2 years to 12 years, have a duration of 6.54 years.[11] Using the procedure outlined above, the risk-management department determines that the $30 million notional principal can be hedged by selling 152 T-note futures. This calculation is:

$$\text{Face Value of Hedge} = \frac{3.15}{6.54} \times \frac{1.00}{0.95} \times \$30 \text{ million} = \$15.21 \text{ million}$$

$$\text{Number of Futures} = \$15.21 \text{ million} \div \$0.1 \text{ million} \approx 152$$

The risk-management group immediately makes the necessary transactions. The bank is now hedged until a matched swap can be arranged. At 9:48, the risk-management department is notified that a second swap has been negotiated. The swap is for $15 million for three years. Like the first, the bank is again the fixed-rate receiver. The risk managers determine that this second swap can be hedged

by selling 43 T-note futures. This is done immediately, and the bank
is now short 195 T-note futures. At 10:23, the risk-management group
is notified that a third swap has been negotiated. This one is a $25
million six-year swap, and the bank is the fixed-rate payer. Because
the maturity of this swap is different from the first two, it is not
regarded as a matched swap. All three swaps are thus carried as
unmatched. The risk managers determine that this swap can be hedged
by purchasing 153 futures, and the transactions are effected immediately. The bank's futures position is thus reduced to a short position
in 42 T-note futures. At 10:52 AM, the risk-management group is notified
that a $20 million 4-year swap with the bank as fixed-rate payer
has been negotiated. This swap is regarded as a partial match for
the first swap. The hedge for the fourth swap requires the purchase
of 71 futures. The transactions are effected immediately, and the
bank is now long 29 T-note futures. These trades are summarized in
Exhibit 4.14 which is a small portion of the bank's daily risk-
management report.

EXHIBIT 4.14

RISK-MANAGEMENT REPORT

Time	Bank is Fixed Rate Payer(-) Receiver(+) Notional Principal	Maturity	—— Short(-) Long(+) —— Futures Hedge	Net Futures Position
09:15 AM	+ 30.0 million	4 years	- 152	- 152
09:48 AM	+15.0 million	3 years	- 43	- 195
10:23 AM	- 25.0 million	6 years	+ 153	- 42
10:52 AM	- 20.0 million	4 years	+ 71	+ 29

A swap bank which makes a market in currency swaps might
hedge its foreign-exchange risk using currency futures in a fashion
similar to that used by the swap bank above to hedge its interest-
rate risk. Other instruments which can be used to hedge interest-rate
and currency exposures include options, forward contracts, forward
rate contracts (FRAs), and forward exchange contracts (FXAs). The
latter two instruments were briefly discussed in Chapter 2.

Managing Credit Risk

Credit risk is not a hedgeable risk. Fortunately, as discussed earlier,
it is easily diversified away. Nevertheless, the swap bank must in-

clude provisions to protect itself from individual defaults. Failure to do so would increase the likelihood of defaults which are in the financial interests of the bank's counterparties. For credit risk to be fully diversified away, the likelihood of defaults which injure the bank and the likelihood of defaults which benefit the bank must equal.

There are a number of ways that banks can protect themselves from credit risk. These include (1) including "events of default" provisions in the swap agreement which provide for appropriate payments to cover damages resulting from early termination of the swap agreement, (2) improving the creditworthiness of the counterparty through credit enhancements, (3) reducing the size of the credit risk by set-off with existing counterparties, (4) passing the credit risk to another party by assignment of the swap. We consider each of these briefly in turn.

All swap contracts include termination clauses which provide for the assessment of damages in the event that one party to a swap should default. These clauses detail the various "events of default," "termination events," and the process for "measuring damages." The latter is one of the most important clauses in a swap agreement, and it is not surprising that the ISDA's code of swaps devotes more space to detailing the available options for measuring and assessing damages in the event of a default or early termination than it does to almost any other single issue.

In the early days of swap contracting, swap banks employed a variety of *ad hoc* methods for measuring and assessing damages. In 1985, the ISDA introduced its first code of swaps which helped standardize swap contracts and which provided several detailed methods for assessing damages in the event of default or early termination. This standardization process continued with a 1986 revision of the code and culminated in 1987 with the publication of the ISDA's standard form agreements. The ISDA's standards provide several alternative methods for determining settlement payments upon early termination. Critical to each of these methods are the concepts of **defaulting party** and **affected party**. A defaulting party is a counterparty which has committed an event of default. An affected party is a counterparty which has suffered a termination event. Events of default and termination events are discussed in Chapter 5.

The ISDA's 1986 code provided three basic methods for measuring and assessing damages from defaults and early terminations: **agreement value method**, **indemnification method**, and **formula method**. The agreement value method provides for damages to be determined on the basis of "market quotations" obtained by the nondefaulting party. The market quotation is an amount (which may be negative) determined on the basis of quotations from reference swap market makers equal to the replacement cost of the swap. The indemnification method provides for assessment of damages on the basis of the "loss" resulting from default or early termination. The code provides details for determining the amount of "loss." The formula method provides for the calculation of a lump-sum payment based on a hypothetical series of borrowings and investings in short-term instruments so as to replicate the cash flows associated with the swap. The calculation produces a "formula settlement amount." The payment is then equal to the excess, if any, of the formula settlement amount of the defaulting party over the formula settlement amount of the nondefaulting party. The formula settlement method is rarely used today and only then in certain special situations. In the years since the 1986 code was released, the agreement value method has become nearly universal.

Under all three damage assessment methods the parties may select options to provide for one-way payments, two-way payments, or limited two-way payments. In the one-way payment option, the defaulting or affected party makes payment to the nondefaulting party of the amount required (based on the assessment method selected) if that sum is greater than zero. No payment is made if the sum is less than zero. In the two-way payment option, each party is required to make payment to the other irrespective of which party has defaulted or is affected. These payments are based on the extent to which the assessment amounts exceed zero. In a limited two-way payment option, the one-way payment method applies in cases of an event of default, while the two-way payment method applies in cases of a termination event. Thus, a termination clause may require payments in either direction (from the party who is benefited to the party who is injured by the early termination) regardless of which party is responsible for the default, or, the clause may specify that only the defaulting party shall be required to make a close-out payment.

The principal problem with payments required under termination provisions is that this protection is likely to fail if the default is associated with a counterparty's bankruptcy. In such an event, the counterparty may not be in a position to pay the required indemnity and, indeed, may be stayed from making payment by the bankruptcy laws of its country. Further, even when payment is effected, it will likely be at less than full face value.

The second way to manage credit risk is to improve the creditworthiness of the counterparty through credit enhancements. The simplest form of credit enhancement is for the bank to require that the counterparty pledge collateral. The value of the collateral should be at least equal to the bank's credit (or default) exposure. The credit exposure will change over time as market conditions evolve. The posting of collateral equal to the mark-to-market replacement cost of the swap contract is the most appealing of such approaches. A variation of this same approach is for the swap agreement to call for the posting of collateral in the event that the counterparty's creditworthiness deteriorates.

The third way to manage credit risk is to reduce the exposure by reversing existing swaps. This is most easily accomplished if the existing counterparty is a swap bank. There are a number of ways to structure a reversal. Which way works best in a given situation will depend on the surrounding circumstances. A counterparty may have reasons other than exposure reduction for wanting to reverse a swap: (1) The underlying debt may have been prepaid; (2) the expectation of the parties responsible for the swap may have changed; (3) a very attractive replacement swap has become available; or (4) the swap may have a positive mark-to-market value and the firm would like to reverse the swap to enhance current earnings.

The two basic ways to reverse a swap are to (1) enter a new swap having opposite terms to the original and (2) effect a cancellation by a buy-out. The first approach may be made at market or off-market depending on the behavior of interest rates since the original swap was negotiated. Such a reversal may be effected with the existing counterparty or with an altogether different counterparty. As discussed in Chapter 3, writing an off-market swap will usually involve a buy up or a buy down. The payments on these swaps can then be netted and the exposure reduced. If the two swaps have been made with the same counterparty, the counterparties may find it convenient to cancel the swaps based on their off-setting nature. The second approach, to engage in a simple buy-out cancellation, involves requesting the counterparty to cancel the swap based on a close-out payment. Swap banks will generally accommodate these requests near replacement cost. Other counterparties may not be so willing because their existing swap is designed to serve some specific corporate purpose.

Consider the following example: A swap bank enters a five-year interest-rate swap as fixed-rate payer with Counterparty A and then matches this commitment as fixed-rate receiver with a swap with Counterparty B. The swap bank records a credit exposure on both swaps. Later, the swap bank enters a five-year interest-rate swap as fixed-rate receiver with Counterparty C and would, normally, look to match this swap with a swap with another counterparty, whom we will call Counterparty D. In the swap with Counterparty D, the bank would be a fixed-rate payer. If the bank does this, it would then have a recorded exposure on four separate swaps. Now, suppose that instead of doing the final swap with Counterparty D, the bank again approaches Counterparty B. Recall that in its first swap with Counterparty B, the bank is the fixed-rate receiver. Since the bank now needs a swap, to match its obligation to Counterparty C, in which the bank is the fixed-rate payer, the bank offers such a swap to Counterparty B. At the same time, the bank requests that the two opposing swaps between the swap bank and Counterparty B cancel one another. As it happens, Counterparty B is amenable to this cancellation. By writing off-setting swaps in this way, the bank reduces its swap exposure from four swaps to two swaps.

Of course, it is highly unlikely that market conditions have remained unchanged since the time the first swap with Counterparty B was written. Thus, the off-setting swaps will not have identical terms nor identical values. This will necessitate a netting of economic values, resulting in a profit or loss for the swap bank (and, of course, a loss or profit for Counterparty B). This closeout will be effected with a single payment from the bank to Counterparty B or by a single payment from Counterparty B to the bank. The value of this closeout payment is approximately the value of writing an off-market swap, as discussed in Chapter 3.

Swap banks often engage in multiple swaps with the same counterparties but not always for the purpose of reversing existing swaps. It is common today for banks that frequently engage in swaps with one another (interbank swaps) to have a **master swap agreement**. Such an agreement is simply a document which governs all swaps between the parties, with each new swap representing a supplement to the master agreement. Such a master agreement would provide for a netting of obligations. Thus, payment flows between the parties are limited to the payment differentials. Banks generally maintain that this netting of obligations reduces their exposure on their swap portfolios and, for internal risk-management purposes, swap banks typically calculate a net exposure to each final institution with which they transact. For purposes of bank regulation of credit exposures, however, it has not yet been decided whether this netting of exposures under master swap agreements will affect bank capital requirements. The recently adopted Federal Reserve rules governing capital requirements and credit exposures are discussed later in this chapter.

The final approach to the management of credit risk is to assign the swap to another party. That is, a booked swap can, theoretically, be **assigned**, and the credit risk transferred in the process. This approach is difficult because it requires the approval of both counterparties to the swap. The uninvolved counterparty may be unwilling to allow its swap to be transferred because that party derives no benefit from the transfer. A solution is to include an assignment clause at the time the swap is written, thus permitting the bank to make such a transfer. These assignments, however, are quite complicated. As a general matter, permissive assignments are not allowed under most swap agreements. Most often assignment is a matter left to subsequent negotiation should interest in an assignment arise.

Miscellaneous Portfolio Management Considerations

There are a great many other considerations in the management of the risks associated with swaps. Many of these become of concern only when specialty swaps are created. For example, a bank may have a difficult time finding a match for a putable or a callable swap. Or, it may find that such a swap can only be matched if the bank buys the necessary provisions from a second counterparty. But, sometimes, different features of different speciality swaps can be offsetting. For example, if the bank grants a floating-rate payer the right to terminate a seven-year swap after four years (a putable swap), the bank might be able to offset the risk by entering a second swap with a four-year maturity as a floating-rate payer and reserving the right to extend the life of the swap for three additional years (an extendable swap).

If the first counterparty elects to "put" its swap with the bank, the bank would simply not extend its swap with the second counterparty. If the first counterparty elects not to "put" its swap with the bank, the bank would extend its swap with the second counterparty.

We have assumed throughout that the bank looks to minimize its risk exposure. This is not necessarily a realistic assumption. Some swap banks take speculative positions in swaps. That is, they carry a portion of their swap portfolio unhedged, or they deliberately mismatch specific swap provisions in an effort to exploit their expectations as to the likely course of interest rates, spreads between different rate indexes, the future shape of the yield curve, and so on. These decisions are typically made by experienced management teams backed up by the bank's research department.

The Treatment of Swaps under the New International Capital Standards

Many of the institutions which act as market makers in swaps are commercial banks. These banks were attracted to the swap market because swaps allowed them to enhance their return on equity. This opportunity to increase profitability was possible because swaps are off-balance sheet transactions. That is, swaps do not appear on either the asset or the liability side of a balance sheet.

Despite the considerable amount of deregulation in the banking industry over the last 10 years, banking is still one of the most highly regulated of all industries. There is a public interest in maintaining the soundness of the banking system. For this reason, banks are subject to a great number of regulatory controls. One of the most important of these controls is the requirement that banks, and bank holding companies, maintain satisfactory levels of bank capital. All other things being equal, banks would prefer to count both long-term debt and equity as capital, while bank regulators would prefer to count only equity. Debt allows the firm to leverage itself and, in so doing, increase the return to its shareholders.

Capital provides a cushion for depositors in the event that the bank suffers operating losses and/or some of the bank's assets lose value. Historically, the capital requirement was determined as a percentage of bank assets. But, because swaps provide a source of earnings for banks without increasing bank assets, swap activity did not increase capital requirements. Thus, swaps were seen as a way to enhance shareholder returns. As swaps became a progressively larger portion of bank business for many large banks, bank regulators became increasingly concerned about the adequacy of bank capital under the existing capital requirements. They believed that swaps exposed banks to risks which conventional risk measures ignored.

On several occasions, bank regulators made capital adequacy proposals to correct what they perceived to be a dangerous situation. Many of the proposals were extreme. For example, some early proposals would have imposed capital requirements on notional swap principal equal to the requirements imposed on a straight loan. Such proposals demonstrated a lack of understanding of the swap product. As we have shown in this chapter, the default risk on a swap (in which cash flows pass in two directions) is considerably less than the default risk on a straight loan having an equal principal (in which cash flows pass in only one direction).

A second argument made by U.S. banksagainst the imposition of new capital requirements dealt with the global nature of the swap market. Banks maintained that stiff capital requirements on swaps would force them to increase their bid-asked spread on the swaps in which they make a market in order to cover their increased costs. This increase in the bid-asked spread for domestic swap banks would place them at a competitive disadvantage to nondomestic swap banks. The swap business would then simply move overseas--mostly to London. The banks further argued that, if the U.S. was to remain a leader in international finance, it could not afford to so easily surrender to its foreign competition.

These arguments proved persuasive. As a first step, the Federal Reserve, together with the Bank of England, issued proposals calling for risk-based capital requirements. These were put out for public comment during 1986 and 1987. Subsequently, the Federal Reserve sent representatives to Basle Switerland to work with representatives of the central banking authorities of the Group of Ten plus Luxembourg.[12] This group became known as the **Basle Supervisors' Committee**, and in December of 1987, it agreed to a set of principles dealing with the definition of bank capital and new risk-based capital requirements. This set of principles became known as the **Basle Accord**. The Basle Accord standardized bank capital requirements across nations and removed the argument that stiffer swap capital requirements would unfairly impact on U.S. banks.

After a period of public comment, the Federal Reserve issued final guidelines on January 19, 1989. These guidelines were designed to achieve several important goals:[13]

- Establishment of a uniform capital framework, applicable to all federally supervised banking organizations.
- Encouragement of international banking organizations to strengthen their capital positions.
- Reduction of a source of competitive inequality arising from differences in supervisory requirements among nations.

The Fed's new guidelines encompass a great deal besides swap activity. Indeed, the guidelines impose risk-adjusted capital requirements based on all off-balance sheet and on-balance sheet activities which contribute to a bank's risk exposure. We are concerned here, however, only with swaps.

The procedure for assessing capital requirements for a swap is a four-step process: The first step is to determine the notional principal on the swap. Based on this notional principal, the swap coupon, and the prevailing level of interest rates, the swap is marked-to-market and the replacement cost of the swap ascertained. To this replacement cost, an additional amount is added on to account for future volatility. This "add-on" factor ranges from 0 percent to 5 percent depending on the type of swap and the term of the swap. The result of these calculations is called the **credit risk equivalent**. Ascertaining this value constitutes the second step. The third step involves a risk weighting. This requires a simple multiplication of the credit risk equivalent by a fixed percentage. The percentage itself depends on the general quality of the creditor. For example, a swap with a central government within the Organization of Economic Cooperation and Development (OECD) involves a risk-factor of 0 percent. At the other extreme is a swap negotiated with a corporation, a nonbank financial institution, or a bank incorporated outside of the OECD. For swaps with these institutions, the risk factor is 50 percent. This multiplication yields a value called the "risk-weighted asset." The final step is to determine the capital requirement by multiplying the risk-weighted asset by the capital ratio. The Basle Accord set this at 8 percent, and this ratio was later adopted by the Federal Reserve.

It would clearly help to run through an example. Suppose a swap bank negotiates a four-year interest-rate swap with a domestic corporation having a notional principal of $50 million. Because the swap is an interest-rate swap with a term of more than 1 year, the "add on" factor will be 0.5 percent of the notional principal. When the swap is first written, the swap is at market and has a mark-to-market value of $0. When the "add on" of $0.25 million (0.005 x $50 million) is included, the swap is found to have a credit risk equivalent of $0.25 million. The risk weight for this swap is 50 percent, so the risk-weighted asset is $0.125 million. Since the capital ratio is 8 percent, the capital requirement is $10,000. Thus, the bank must keep $10,000 of capital to support this particular swap. As interest rates change, the swap will be repeatedly marked-to-market with the result that the capital requirement is repeatedly changing. Suppose, for example that interest rates rise and the swap is found to have a replacement cost of $50,000. The bank's capital requirement for this swap would rise to $12,000. These calculations are depicted in Exhibit 4.15.

The guidelines allow for the calculation of replacement cost (through marking-to-market) on the basis of netting provided that the swap agreements governing the swaps provide for mutual cancellation in the event of a default. That is, banks with multiple swaps that allow for netting can calculate the replacement cost of the swap on a net basis. This significantly reduces bank capital requirements relative to what they would otherwise be.

EXHIBIT 4.15

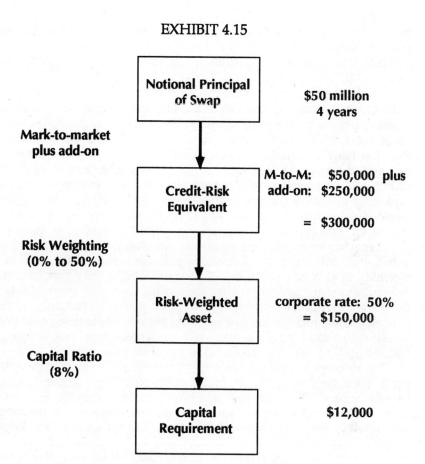

The Fed's guidelines have had a very positive effect on the market. The guidelines reflect the realities of swap risks to market-making banks. They also eliminate a cloud which has hung over the swap market from the outset. Since the Fed's new guidelines were announced, the growth in the market for swaps has accelerated.

Summary

A swap bank holds a portfolio of swaps to earn a return from its bid-asked spread and, to a lesser degree, from front-end fees. While a front-end fee provides an immediate reward for the swap bank for its financial engineering, the return from the bid-asked spread is realized over an extended period of time. To profit from its swap activity, the swap bank must bear risk. A fundamental premise of financial theory is that economic entities (including both individuals and firms) are risk averse. Thus, a key ingredient in successfully running a swap portfolio (swap book) is controlling the various risk exposures associated with the portfolio.

Ideally, the swap bank would perfectly match each swap to which it becomes a counterparty with an offsetting swap with another counterparty. If both swaps could be entered simultaneously and if all of the bank's counterparties were completely free of credit risk, then the bank's portfolio would be riskless. In such a perfect environment, the swap bank would best be viewed as a pure arbitrager—taking riskless positions with no investment and earning a profit by exploiting inefficiencies among the segmented capital markets of the world. Unfortunately, the real world is not nearly so perfect. Swaps are custom designed to meet the end-users' needs, and potential counterparties with matching needs are not always easily found. When found, they often require special swap features that result in a mismatching of at least some swap provisions. Finally, very few potential counterparties are perfect credits. As a consequence of these realities, there are a great many different risks associated with running a swap portfolio. These include interest-rate risk, exchange-rate risk, credit risk, market risk, default risk, mismatch risk, basis risk, spread risk, sovereign risk, and delivery risk. The risks must be identified, measured, and managed.

The risks associated with a swap portfolio are related in complex ways. To some degree, the risks are often offsetting—in the sense of natural hedges. Thus, the risk manager must consider the risk character of the overall portfolio rather than the risk character of the swaps individually. Some risks can be hedged. Others cannot be. When hedging is possible, the risk manager will hedge in futures, options, the Treasury and Eurodollar markets, FRAs, FXAs, and other risk-management vehicles. Hedges of this type must be managed dynamically—placed and lifted as the portfolio evolves over time. The risks that are not hedgeable should be managed in other ways. Some risks, such as credit risks, are unsystematic by nature and can be dramatically reduced by simple diversification. Nevertheless, the bank should reduce these risks as much as possible by providing for replacement compensation in the event of default and by credit enhancements when possible. Other risks, like sovereign risks, are systematic by nature and can best be managed by limiting the firm's exposure in markets where this risk is deemed to be more substantial.

Identifying, measuring, and managing the risks associated with running a swap portfolio are clearly complicated undertakings. Most swap banks maintain a staff of risk-management specialists who are often consulted prior to the writing of a swap. This is particularly important when the swap is complicated by novel provisions with which the bank has little experience.

Terms

affected party
agreement value method (for assessing damages)
assigned
basis
basis risk
Basle Accord
Basle Supervisors' Committee
buy-up (buy-down)
cost of carry
credit risk
credit risk equivalent
date sensitive
default risk
defaulting party
delivery risk
discriminant analysis
dollar value basis point hedging model
downside risk
duration-based hedging model
events of default
formula method (for assessing damages)
indemnification method (for assessing damages)
market risk
marking-to-market
master swap agreement
mismatch risk
natural hedge
netting
perfectly correlated
regression analysis
replacement swap
reset dates
sovereign risk
spread risk
supervening illegality
systematic risk
TED spread
termination events
transfer pricing rate (TPR)
unsystematic risk
volatility

REVIEW QUESTIONS

1. What is the difference between making a market in swaps and using swaps as speculative tools?

2. Suppose a swap bank writes an interest-rate swap on which it is the fixed-rate receiver (floating-rate payer). The swap is a 7-year nonamortizing interest-rate swap having a notional principal of $25 million. The swap coupon is 9.50 percent with payments made semiannually. Now suppose that before the bank can match the swap with a second counterparty, the bank's midrate for swaps of this maturity increases by 18 basis points. By how much has the present value of the bank changed and in which direction?

3. Suppose that a bank has determined that a potential counterparty has a credit risk (probability of default) of 1.5 percent. This same client would like to negotiate a swap with the bank. The bank determines that the market risk to the bank in the event of default on this swap is $1,750,000. What is the bank's default risk on this swap?

4. Explain why a mismatch of swap terms exposes a swap bank to some risks.

5. Why does a swap bank consider all of its relationships with clients in a given foreign country, not just its swap relationships, in setting acceptable levels of sovereign risk?

6. Explain the source of delivery risk. How might a bank manage this risk?

7. Suppose that a swap is determined to have a duration of 4.5 years. The Tresury-note futures in which the fixed-rate side of the swap will be hedged has a duration of 6.25 years. These Tresury-note futures are currently priced at 94.25 percent of par. Each futures contract covers $0.1 million of face value notes. The swap has a notional principal of $12 million, and the bank is the fixed-rate payer. Determine the number of T-note futures the bank would have to buy (sell) to fully hedge the fixed-rate side of this swap.

8. Discuss the ways a swap bank can protect itself from credit risk.

9. Suppose a swap bank enters a 15-year $20 million interest-rate swap with itself as fixed-rate payer. The swap coupon is a semi-annual 8.80 percent. Further, suppose that rates decline so that a week later new swaps of similar term are being written with

midrates of 8.60 percent (the bank adds or subtracts 10 bps to the midrate depending on whether it is fixed-rate receiver or fixed-rate payer). Determine the mark-to-market value of this swap.

10. Assuming that the swap described in Problem 9 above was made with a corporation and that the capital ratio is 8 percent, determine the amount of capital the bank must hold to support this particular swap.

ENDNOTES

1. In the context of modern portfolio theory, the risk associated with holding an investment portfolio can be divided into two types: systematic and unsystematic. **Unsystematic risk** is that risk which is unique to the individual asset. This risk is easily diversified away. **Systematic risk** is that portion of the asset's risk which is correlated to the behavior of the general market. Systematic risk is measured with the aid of beta coefficients. An asset's beta is the ratio of its covariance of return with the market to the variance of the rate of return on the market as a whole. A fuller discussion of systematic risk, unsystematic risk, and beta measurement can be found in Haugen (1986). In the context of hedging theory with futures, a fuller discussion can be found in Marshall (1989, Chapters 6 and 7).

2. More precisely, the yield level is a function of duration. However, since maturity is the primary determinant of duration, we adopt the standard convention of discussing yields relative to maturities rather than yields relative to durations. For a more complete discussion of this point, see Chapter 3.

3. When swaps were first introduced, the market makers' bid-asked spread would often run to a 100 basis points or more. Intense competition has reduced the spreads to no more than 20 basis points and usually substantially less.

4. This issue has been examined by Winder (1986).

5. **Regression analysis** and **discriminant analysis** are multivariate forecasting techniques which have been used to determine which financial ratios or combinations of financial ratios are most reliable at predicting business failure. As such, these tools are useful for assessing the creditworthiness of a client firm. For a more detailed discussion of these techniques and their application in measuring creditworthiness, see Foster (1986) and Altman (1983).

Factor analysis has also been used for this purpose. For a discussion of this technique, see Chen and Shimerda (1981). For a discussion of the measurement of credit risk in the context of swap finance, see Cooper (1987).

6. The credit risks (probabilities of default) used in this example are considerably higher than those typical in actual practice. For example, a 1987-88 survey by the ISDA of 71 swap dealers showed that only 11 had ever experienced any write-offs of notional principal. These write-offs amounted to $33.0 million on aggregate portfolios of $283.0 billion—equivalent to about 1/100th of 1 percent.

7. Becoming increasingly common is a process of marking contracts to market (i.e., determining replacement cost) and requiring the counterparties to post collateral equal to this mark-to-market value. The First Boston Corporation was the first swap dealer to adopt a mutual mark-to-market collateral provision in its swap master agreements.

8. This assumes that there is equal likelihood of a counterparty's default whether interest rates rise or fall. This assumption would be violated if the fixed-rate paying counterparties become increasingly likely to default when interest rates fall or if fixed-rate receiving counterparties become increasingly likely to default when interest rates rise. The violation of the assumption, however, does not alter the conclusion. It only mitigates, to some degree, the strength of the conclusion.

9. The term "basis" is used in hedging theory to mean the difference between two prices. These prices need not be interest rates. They can just as easily be exchange rates, commodity prices, etc. Basis risk is the risk that the two prices will evolve differently. Basis risk is measured as the variance of the basis. A hedge is considered effective if the basis risk is less than the price risk. For a thorough discussion of basis risk in the context of futures hedging, see Marshall (1989, Chapter 7).

10. Many swap banks prefer the **dollar value basis point model** to hedging interest-rate exposure. It can be shown, however, that, if properly used, a duration-based hedging model, adjusted for yield-change differences, and the dollar value basis point hedging model will produce the same hedge outcomes. For a derivation and discussion of the dollar value basis point model and its relationship to the duration model, see Marshall (1989, Chapter 12).

11. Futures themselves have no duration, but they behave exactly as though they have a duration identical to that of the underlying

instrument. For this reason, we calculate the duration of the T-note on which the futures is written and then treat this duration as the duration of the T-note futures. The same would apply if we were using T-bill or T-bond futures as the hedging instrument. Importantly, the underlying instrument must be taken to be the "cheapest-to-deliver" alternative permissible on the futures. For a further discussion of this point, see Gay and Kolb (1984).

12. The Group of Ten is Belgium, Canada, France, Germany, Italy, Japan, the Netherlands, Sweden, Switzerland, the United Kingdom, and the United States.

13. See Federal Reserve Press Release dated January 19, 1989 to accompany Risk-Based Capital Guidelines.

REFERENCES AND SUGGESTED READINGS

Altman, E. I. *Corporate Financial Distress.* (New York: Wiley, 1983).

Chen, K. H. and T. A. Shimerda. "An Empirical Analysis of Useful Financial Ratios." *Financial Management* (Spring 1981).

Commins, K. "Risk Management: The Eight Best Hedges." *Intermarket,* 4:8, 17-23 (August 1987).

Cooper, D. F. and Watson, I. R. "How to Assess Credit Risks in Swaps." *Banker,* 137:732, 28-31 (February 1987).

Felgran, S. D. "Interest Rate Swaps: Use, Risk, and Prices." *New England Economic Review* (Federal Reserve Bank of Boston), 22-32 (November/December 1987).

Foster, G. *Financial Statement Analysis,* 2d ed. (Englewood Cliffs, N.J.: Prentice-Hall 1986).

Gay, G. D. and R. W. Kolb. "Removing Bias in Duration Based Hedging Models: A Note." *Journal of Futures Markets,* 4:2, 225-228 (Summer 1984).

Haugen, R. A. *Modern Investment Theory* (Englewood Cliff, N.J.: Prentice-Hall, 1986).

Henderson, S. K. "Termination Provisions of Swap Agreements." *International Financial Law Review (UK),* 22-27 (September 1983).

Hyde, J. H. "A Swap Torpedo." *United States Banker,* 98:10, 36-40 (October 1987).

Marshall, J. F. *Futures and Option Contracting* (Cincinnati: South-Western Publishing Co., 1989).

Miller, G. "When Swaps Unwind." *Institutional Investor*, 20:11, 165-178 (November 1986).

Smith, D. J. "Measuring the Gains from Arbitraging the Swap Market." *Financial Executive*, 4:2, 46-49 (March/April 1988).

Stoakes, C. "How to Terminate A Swap." *Euromoney*, (April 1985).

Winder, R. "The Art of Exposure Management." *Euromoney*, 51-54 (April 1986).

CHAPTER 5

SWAP DOCUMENTATION

Overview

Swaps are typically initiated through telephone conversations. The initial agreement usually hinges on a few key economic issues such as the swap coupon, the floating rate, the payment frequency, and the maturity. The verbal agreement is confirmed by a telex or letter (called the confirmation), usually within 24 hours. While both parties are legally bound by the initial agreement, it is still far from complete. Complete documentation, which is extensive, is exchanged later. The swap documentation must cover all terms agreed to in the initial exchange but must also cover a great many incidental issues, including many noneconomic issues that bear on the relationship between the counterparties. These would include such things as events of default, methods of computing damages on an early termination, jurisdiction governing disputes, and so forth.

In the early days of swap finance, each swap bank chose its own wording for all of its swap contract documentation. Variations in the phrasing of this documentation and differing definitions of certain terms necessitated careful review by each counterparty's legal counsel. As a consequence, the lack of standardization introduced potentially injurious delays in the approval of the contracts, as well as unnecessarily large legal expenses. Lack of standardization also made it potentially difficult for swap banks to match swaps and limited swap market participants' ability to trade swaps in a well-defined secondary market and to reverse swaps with existing counterparties.

A limited amount of standardized wording began to spontaneously emerge as banks found it efficient and economical to reuse the same (or similar) clauses in swaps having similar terms. Banks also found it convenient to pirate one another's clauses as new features found their way into swap contracts. Despite this evolution, however, standardization remained elusive.

Most of the operatives in the swap banking industry eventually came to recognize that it was in the interests of all participants to work toward standardization. As a first effort, a small group of representatives from some of the leading swap banks began working on standardization of documentation in 1984. In March of 1985, this group, now expanded, organized itself as the New York based International Swap Dealers Association (ISDA). Then, in June of 1985, the ISDA released its first code of swaps: *The Code of Standard Wording, Assumptions and Provisions for Swaps*, 1985 edition. The 1985 Code addressed two key issues: (1) the cash flows of a rate swap, including the specification and calculation of the fixed- and floating-rate sides, and (2) the amounts payable upon an early termination of the swap. The ISDA code proved appealing and was soon adopted, in whole or in part, by most U.S. swap dealers. During this same period, the London-based British Bankers' Association (BBA) was working on its own code of swaps; and in August of 1985, the BBA introduced its documentation guidelines—the *British Bankers Association's Interest Rate Swaps* or BBAIRS. The BBA's code was intended primarily as a documentation aid for interbank swaps. While BBAIRS is important, particularly for British banks, this chapter focuses on the more successful standardization efforts of the ISDA.

The ISDA's 1985 Code was only the first step in its efforts at standardizing the language and provisions of swap documentation. In 1986, the ISDA released a revised and expanded version of the code (**1986 Code**). Like the 1985 version, this version devotes considerable attention to defining the cash flows associated with rate swaps and the amounts payable upon early termination. But the 1986 Code refines these provisions to facilitate the development of integrated master swap agreements. The 1986 Code also addresses a number of other issues to which the 1985 Code had been silent. In particular, the 1986 Code devotes considerable attention to the subjects of "events of default" and "termination events." The 1986 Code also provides a list of representations made by the parties to the swap, a list of agreements pertaining to information to be furnished on an ongoing basis, definitions pertaining to specific entities when a swap is guaranteed or supported by an entity other than the actual counterparty, cross-border provisions, and withholding tax provisions.

In 1987, the ISDA took another giant step toward standardization of documentation by introducing standard form agreements. There are two versions of the standard form agreements. The first is a code-based form called the "**Interest Rate Swap Agreement.**" It is an agreement for U.S. dollar denominated swaps, and it incorporates the 1986 Code by reference, with certain modifications. The second is a multicurrency form called the "**Interest Rate and Currency Exchange Agreement.**" This form covers interest-rate swaps in any currency, as well as currency swaps and cross-currency interest-rate swaps. The Interest Rate and Currency Exchange Agreement does not reference the code directly but incorporates provisions which are virtually identical to those in the 1986 Code. Certain provisions of the Code, Articles 2 through 8, which describe how fixed and floating payments are to be calculated and which provide various floating-rate options, are not included in this standard form. These issues are, instead, addressed through separate confirmations. To assist in the addressing of these issues, the ISDA also released in 1987 a document called the *1987 Interest Rate and Currency Exchange Definitions.*

In this chapter, we provide an overview of the standard form agreements; and we introduce a number of terms defined in the 1986 Code, many of which have not been used elsewhere in this book. The reader is cautioned that many of the terms have subtle legal meanings that we have made no attempt to capture in this brief review. Documentation is a complex legal affair, and any party to it should consult expert counsel. Copies of the 1986 Code, the Standard Form Agreements, and the *1987 Interest Rate and Currency Exchange Definitions* may be obtained, at modest cost, from the ISDA at the following address:

International Swap Dealers Association
1 Rockefeller Plaza, Suite 1505
New York, NY   10020

The ISDA can also provide some empirical data to assist those interested in studying this important market in greater depth.

The Standard Form Agreements

While the 1985 and 1986 ISDA codes greatly enhanced the standardization of swap documentation, neither is, in and of itself, a contract. The codes simply provide standard definitions, presumptions that apply unless specifically overridden, and a menu of options for dealing with certain matters. The existence of a code does not eliminate the need for parties to a swap to develop and execute contracts, although the contracts they develop would, logically, reference the Code.

To standardize the actual contracts, the ISDA published standard form agreements in 1987. As already noted, these agreements are of two types: an "Interest Rate Swap Agreement" (U.S. dollar code-based form) and an "Interest Rate and Currency Exchange Agreement" (multicurrency form). Shortly thereafter, the ISDA published a document called the *1987 Interest Rate and Currency Exchange Definitions* that contains many of the same provisions found in the 1986 Code. The currency exchange definitions are intended to be used with the multicurrency form. The publication provides definitions and rules for computing floating-rate payments for fifteen different currencies.

The ISDA's standard form agreements are designed to be master swap agreements. Each agreement consists of a set of standard terms applicable to any swap transaction together with an accompanying schedule which allows the parties to tailor the agreement by listing terms specific to swaps between the two parties.

As master agreements, the swap documentation governs all subsequent swaps between the parties by simple reference to the master agreement. Each new swap becomes a supplement to the existing master agreement and, consequently, the swap parties can limit their negotiation on each new swap to those matters of economic importance. This minimizes the likelihood that disagreements will develop later over the terms of the swap, and it greatly speeds execution for parties that frequently transact swaps with one another. As discussed in the last chapter, master agreements can provide for a netting of exposures and, hence, the recording of exposures on a net basis. The agreements provide that all swap transactions governed by the master agreement are simultaneously terminated if either party should default on any swap transaction governed by the master agreement. This prevents a bankruptcy trustee from selectively enforcing those swaps which have a positive mark-to-market value, while discarding those swaps having negative mark-to-market value. As of this writing, however, the Federal Reserve has not yet taken a final position on whether this netting of exposures will be applicable to the determination of bank capital requirements under its new capital guidelines.

The two versions of the standard form agreements (i.e., the code-based U.S. dollar version and the multicurrency version) employ the same basic ordering of provisions and, for the most part, the same numbering of their sections. The first section provides for the identification of the parties to the swap. This is followed by sections dealing with payments, representations, agreements, events of default and termination events, early termination, transfer, multibranch provisions, notices, tax matters, credit support documentation, governing law and jurisdiction, definitions, and confirmations.

Payments

Most payment terms are specific to the swap and, therefore, specified in the accompanying schedule. The standard terms provide for the netting of payments on a given swap when payments between the parties are to be made on the same date and in the same currency. As an extension, the agreement provides that the parties net payments on different swaps between them when those payments are to be made on the same date and in the same currency.

Representations

This section contains representations and warranties which each party to the swap makes to the other. The representations and warranties are deemed to be repeated with each new swap entered that is governed by the master agreement. The "basic representations" concern corporate authority to enter into the swap agreement and the validity of the agreement. Other representations include the "absence of certain events," such as the occurrence of an event of default or a termination event, the "absence of litigation" that might threaten the legality, validity, or enforceability of the contract, the "accuracy of financial information," and the "accuracy of specific information" that is furnished in writing by one party to the other.

Agreements

This section provides for supplemental agreements to furnish documents, excluding tax covenants in the code-based form, as detailed by the parties in the accompanying schedule to the master agreement. These might include such things as the periodic furnishing of financial statements or legal opinions, the provision of "credit support documentation," or other documents.

Events of Default and Termination Events

This section deals with "events of default" and "termination events." Events of default indicate that a credit problem has arisen and entitle the nondefaulting party to terminate all swaps governed by the master agreement.

Termination events are due to occurrences other than credit problems and allow for the termination of those swaps directly affected by the termination event. The agreements provide for seven specific events of default, but the parties may specify others if they like. The specific events of default, most of which apply to both parties, are: failure to pay, breach of covenant, credit support default, misrepresentation, default under specified swaps, cross default, and bankruptcy. **Failure to pay** refers to any failure by either party to pay an amount required under the agreement. A **breach of covenant**, as an event of default, refers to a failure to comply with any covenant of the swap agreement other than the making of a required payment, a tax-related matter, or a failure to give notice that a termination event has occurred. **Credit support default** refers to any default under an applicable credit support document. It only applies to a party if a credit support document is required by that party or on behalf of that party. **Misrepresentation** refers to a breach of any representation (other than a tax representation) made in the swap agreement or credit support documentation. **Default under specified swaps** refers to a default that results in the designation or occurrence of a termination event under another swap. **Cross default** refers to a default on some other indebtedness. This event of default can be applied to both parties, only one party, or excluded entirely from the swap agreement by so indicating in the accompanying schedule. The **bankruptcy** event of default is broadly defined to allow for significant variations in the bankruptcy and insolvency laws of the countries covered by the swap agreement.

The agreement specifies certain termination events. These are illegality, a tax event, a tax event upon merger, and a credit event upon merger. An **illegality** is deemed to have occurred if a change in law or regulation makes it impossible for either party to perform its obligations. A **tax event** occurs if a withholding tax is imposed on a swap transaction. In this event, the party required to pay the tax may opt to terminate the swap. A **tax event upon merger** occurs if a merger results in the imposition of a withholding tax on one or more swaps. Only those affected swaps may be terminated. A **credit**

event upon merger occurs if a merger results in a deterioration of the creditworthiness of one of the parties. In such an event, the other party may elect to terminate all swaps governed by the master agreement.

Early Termination

Upon the occurrence of an event of default, the nondefaulting party has the right to designate an "**early termination date.**" In the case of bankruptcy, the termination is automatic. With the exception of bankruptcy, the nondefaulting party must provide notice to the defaulting party as to the early termination date.

In the case of the occurrence of a terminating event, the party who is entitled to designate an early termination date varies with the nature of the terminating event.

As previously mentioned, in the case of an event of default, all swaps governed by the same master agreement are terminated. In the case of a termination event, only the affected swaps are terminated.

Once a notice of early termination has become effective, each party to a terminated swap is released from its obligation to make its required payments under the swap. The parties must then calculate **termination payments.** The options available to the parties were discussed in Chapter 4. They include the agreement value method, the indemnification method, and the formula method. As also discussed in Chapter 4, the agreement value method has become nearly universal. The payments may be made on a one-way basis, a two-way basis, or a limited two-way basis.

Transfer

This section of the agreements provides a general prohibition against the **transfer** of rights and obligation under the agreement to other parties. Allowance is made for specifying exceptions to this general prohibition. These exceptions must be detailed in the accompanying schedule. This is the general prohibition against permissive assignment discussed in Chapter 4.

Multibranch Provisions

This section of the agreements allows institutions with multiple branches which operate from several locations to govern all swaps with a single master agreement.

Notices

This section requires that addresses and telex numbers for purposes of providing required **notices** be specified in the accompanying schedule. All notices provided must be in writing and sent to the required address or telex.

Tax Matters

The tax section of the agreements deals with three tax issues: gross up, tax representation, and tax covenants. As a general rule, counterparties are required to make their payments without any withholding or deductions for taxes. However, if a party making a payment is legally required to withhold taxes from the payment, the party making the payment is required to gross up the amount of the payment for any amount withheld on account of "indemnifiable taxes." The party is, however, released from its **tax gross up** obligation if the withholding is the result of a breach of a tax-related representation or covenant made by the other party. The parties must specify all applicable tax representations in the accompanying schedule and must agree to give notice of breaches of tax representation (tax covenants).

Credit Support Documentation

The parties should identify in the accompanying schedule all required **credit support documents**. These include such things as guarantees, security agreements, and letters of credit.

Governing Law and Jurisdiction

The agreements require that the parties must specify in the accompanying schedule whether New York law or English law will govern the agreements.

Definitions

This section of the agreements defines the following terms: business day, default rate, interest on unpaid amounts, interest on termination payments, and specified entities. We will define the term "business day" in the next section of this chapter. The **"default rate"** is the rate of interest, compounded daily, paid by a defaulting party to a nondefaulting party on any unpaid amounts. The nondefaulting party pays a lower rate of interest on any unpaid amounts. In the case of a terminating event, both parties pay a rate of interest lower than the default rate on the amount of their respective termination payments from the early termination date to the due date. The term **"specified entities"** means different things in different contexts. In each of the contexts in which it is used, the parties must specify the term's meaning in the accompanying schedule.

Confirmations

The agreements require the exchange of **confirmations** detailing the terms of each new swap entered under the master agreement. In the code-based form, intended for U.S. dollar interest-rate swaps only, these confirmations must specify the notional amount, the trade date, the effective date, the termination date, the fixed-rate payer, the fixed-rate payment dates, the fixed amount of each payment, the floating-rate payer, the floating-rate payment dates, the floating rate for the initial calculation period, the floating-rate option, the designated maturity, the spread (plus or minus), floating rate day count fraction, the rest dates (compounding, if applicable), and certain other terms as appropriate.

In the multicurrency form, all of this same information must be provided, but other information is required as well. This would include such things as the relevant currencies, initial exchange, final exchange, and so forth.

Miscellaneous Definitions

The 1986 Code defines a great many terms used in swap documentation. Some of the more important of these terms, particularly those not used elsewhere in this text, are briefly defined below. The definitions below are not necessarily meant to be precise or complete. The reader requiring more precision should refer to the ISDA documents listed in the references to this chapter.

Bond equivalent yield and **money market equivalent yield**	Yield measures used to standardize rate measures on instruments ordinarily quoted on a bank discount basis.
Business day	Any day other than a Saturday, Sunday, or a day on which commercial banks are required or authorized to be closed in the city of reference. If no city of reference is specified, New York is assumed.
Calculation agent	The swap party (or a third party) designated to determine the applicable floating rate and the corresponding floating- and fixed-rate payments due on the payment dates.
Calculation date	The earliest date for any calculation period for which it is practical for the calculating agent to calculate the payments due on the subsequent payment date.
Calculation period	The period beginning on one period end date and ending on the day just prior to the next period end date.
Designated maturity	Is the period of time specified as such.
Dollar	A unit of lawful currency of the United States.
Early termination date	A business day on which the parties to a swap will settle via a lump-sum payment following an event of default or a termination event.
Effective date	Is the date specified as the first date of the term of the swap.
Eurodollar convention	Describes the process for determining payment dates for each payment

period. This determination of dates requires allowance for nonbanking days in New York and London.

Fixed amount

The amount payable by a fixed-rate payer on a payment date.

Floating amount

The amount payable by a floating-rate payer on a payment date.

Gross payment

The full amount of any required payment. When gross payments are specified, each party is required to make full payment of all amounts due to the other party.

London banking day

Any day in which dealings in dollars are transacted in the London interbank market.

Net payment

The difference between the payments made by the counterparties to a swap. When net payments are specified only the higher paying counterparty is required to make a payment. The paying party's payment is equal to the difference between the two parties' gross payments. In the absence of any specification, net payments are assumed.

New York banking day

Any day, other than a Saturday, Sunday, or other day on which commercial banks in New York are required or authorized to be closed.

Notional amount

The amount specified as such for purposes of calculating the floating- and fixed-rate payments.

Payment date

A date that a payment is due. Options allow for delayed payment and early payment. In the event that a payment date would otherwise fall on a non-banking day in either New York or London, options can be included to allow for payments to be made on a "following banking day," a "modified following banking day," or a "preceding day" basis.

Period end dates

Dates on which payment periods end. These may or may not correspond to the payment dates.

Rate cut-off date

The last date used in the determination of the relevant rate. The rate cut-off date must precede the period end date for a payment period.

Reference amount

An amount that is representative for a single transaction in the relevant market at the relevant time.

Reference banks

Banks, selected by the calculation agent, in either the London interbank market or New York City, as appropriate, from which rate quotations are obtained in arriving at the relevant rate. Reference banks are used to obtain rates when the floating rate involves LIBOR or prime.

Reference dealers

Dealers selected by the calculation agent for purposes of determining the relevant rate when the floating rate is Treasury bill, certificate of deposit, commercial paper, Federal funds, or bankers acceptances.

Relevant rate

The applicable value for the floating-rate side of a rate swap. The relevant rate is always stated on an annual basis. The relevant rate is determined by prevailing rates on one or more reset dates. The relevant rate may involve a spread over (under) the prevailing rate.

Reset dates

Specified dates on which the relevant rate is set for the next payment period. When more than one reset date is specified, an averaging of the prevailing rates may be required.

Spread

An amount added to (if positive) or subtracted from (if negative) the prevailing rate to arrive at the relevant rate.

Term (of swap)

The length of time from the effective date of the swap transaction to the termination date of the swap.

Termination date

The date specified which serves as the last date of the swap agreement.

Trade date

The date on which the parties enter into the rate swap transaction.

Summary

This chapter has provided a general review of the efforts made to standardize swap documentation and language. Standardization has been greatly enhanced by the efforts of the New York-based ISDA and the London-based BBA. This standardization has greatly reduced the time it takes to finalize a swap transaction by treating each new swap as a supplement to a master agreement. Futher, this standardization has reduced the cost of contracting, and it has enhanced the liquidity of the secondary market in swaps.

The ISDA's efforts began with the publication of a 1985 *Code of Standard Wording, Assumptions and Provisions for Swaps*. This effort continued with a 1986 revision of the Code and culminated with the 1987 publication of standard form agreements and accompanying support material.

Terms

1986 Code
absence of certain events
absence of litigation
accuracy of financial information
accuracy of specific information
bankruptcy
basic representations
bond equivalent yield
breach of covenant
business day
calculation agent
calculation date
calculation period
confirmations
credit event upon merger
credit support default
credit support documents
cross default
default rate
default under specific swaps
designated maturity
dollar
early termination
early termination date
effective date
Eurodollar convention
failure to pay
fixed amount
floating amount
gross payment
illegality
Interest Rate and Currency Exchange Agreement
Interest Rate Swap Agreement
London banking day
misrepresentation
money market equivalent yield
net payment
New York banking day
notices
notional amount

payment date
period end date
rate cut-off date
reference amount
reference banks
reference dealers
relevant rate
reset dates
specified entities
spread
tax event
tax event upon merger
tax gross up
term (of swap)
termination date
termination payments
trade date
transfer

REFERENCES AND SUGGESTED READING

Cunningham, D.P. and J.B. Golden. "A Practitioner's Guide to the 1986 Code of Swaps." In *Swap Finance Update*, ed., Boris Antl, London: Euromoney, 1987.

ISDA *1986 Code of Standard Wording, Assumptions and Provisions for Swaps*. International Swap Dealers Association, 1986.

ISDA *User's Guide to the Standard Form Agreements*. 1987 Edition, International Swap Dealers Association, 1987.

ISDA *1987 Interest Rate and Currency Exchange Definitions*. International Swap Dealers Association, 1987.

Genova, G. and D. Thompson. "A Guide to Standard Swap Documentation." *Commercial Lending Review*, vol. 3(2), 44-49 (Spring 1988).

Stoakes, C. "Standards Make Swaps Faster." *Euromoney* (November 1985).

INDEX